CHRISTIAN THEOLOGY IN PLAIN LANGUAGE

Other books by Bruce L. Shelley

Church History in Plain Language
By What Authority
Evangelicalism in America
History of Conservative Baptists
Let's Face It
Four Marks of a Total Christian
The Church: God's People
What Baptists Believe

CHRISTIAN THEOLOGY IN PLAIN LANGUAGE

Bruce L. Shelley

WORD BOOKS
PUBLISHER
WACO, TEXAS

A DIVISION OF
WORD, INCORPORATED

CHRISTIAN THEOLOGY IN PLAIN LANGUAGE

Library of Congress Cataloging in Publication Data

Shelley, Bruce L. (Bruce Leon), 1927–
    Christian theology in plain language.

    Bibliography: p.
    Includes index.
    1. Theology, Doctrinal—Popular works.
I. Title.
BT77.S52 1985   230   85–6415
ISBN 0–8499–0381–5

Unless otherwise indicated, Scripture quotations are from the
Holy Bible, New International Version (NIV). Copyright © 1973,
1978, International Bible Society. Used by permission of
Zondervan Bible Publishers. Scripture quotations marked RSV
are from the Revised Standard Version of the Bible, copyrighted
1946, 1952, © 1971, 1973 by the Division of Christian Education
of the National Council of Churches of Christ in the U.S.A. and
are used by permission. The Scripture quotation marked NASB
is from the New American Standard Bible, © The Lockman Foundation
1960, 1972, 1973, 1975, 1977. Scripture quotations marked KJV
are from the King James Version of the Bible.

567898 FG 987654321

Printed in the United States of America

To
Dean Ralph Covell
and my colleagues at Denver Seminary,
who have made the study of theology
a challenging and rewarding
quest

Contents

Foreword

A number of people have contributed to this book in special ways. Ernest Owen, Editorial Director of Word Books, originally suggested the project over a warm breakfast one snowy December morning. Several years before this conversation the Grace Church in Edina, Minnesota, had invited me to participate in their adult education program. During four weekends with a very supportive class of laymen and laywomen I had pieced together a series of lessons on basic Christian beliefs.

Later, my regular Emmaus Bible Class at Bear Valley Baptist Church in Denver agreed to study these doctrines with me. That gave me a chance to reshape the material and to give it another test in a lay setting. When I had written an early draft of the chapters a number of the couples in the class went a second mile and agreed to read a chapter and to give me their reaction.

During the early months of writing, two of my students, Mark Smith and my son, David Shelley, helped me in the early stages of several of the chapters. Then, at the other end of the process, two of my colleagues at Denver Seminary gave me the benefit of their insights. Robert L. Hubbard, Professor of Old Testament, read the two chapters discussing the God who is above us and with us. And Professor James Cummings read the entire manuscript and offered many helpful suggestions. The last four chapters of the book took on a special meaning for me when I discovered that Jim had read them just hours after his doctor told him he had terminal cancer.

My editing and rewriting load was lightened considerably by Mrs. Denise Duke and Mrs. Doris Haslam who took my disheveled manuscript and put it on diskettes while I was teaching in Brazil. Finally, Floyd Thatcher and Al Bryant of Word Books guided the entire project through the various stages of publishing.

I am deeply grateful for all of these friends, more than these words can express.

Eastertime, 1985
BRUCE L. SHELLEY

Walking Together

Like many American families, ours has always had a dog about our yard. Not only have our dogs been playful companions for our children, they have taught me a number of important lessons. Our current dog, Muffin, I have discovered, has access to messages we human beings simply do not receive. She can be lying contentedly on our family room floor, when she suddenly jumps to her feet, rushes to the back door, only to return to the family room and look at us as though to say, "I want out of here, now!"

As soon as we open the door, she scampers toward the back fence of our yard, barking viciously. Why? She has heard some disturbing message from a world beyond the range of human hearing. She knows some neighborhood cat has invaded her terrain. And out she goes to defend her territory.

Modern scientists have created a host of devices for listening to this world beyond the frontier of human hearing: radio, sonar, radar, ultrasonics. These devices have become so much a part of modern travel, medicine, and communications that we now take them for granted. They should convince us all, however, that the world of our five senses is only a tiny part of reality.

This book is about another world, one beyond the range of all human senses, a world our secular society tries to ignore because we can't buy it or consume it or hoard it. Yet, as we hope to show, it is a world absolutely essential for any sort of meaningful life on Planet Earth. Let's just call it, the Hidden World.

The book's cover, you will find, says nothing about the Hidden World. It speaks, instead, of "Christian Theology." We took some risk in using that title because most people consider "theology" a scary term, something like the names of the drugs a doctor prescribes for an infection. "Theology," however, need not arouse our fears. It stands for something close to each of us, our religious convictions. It comes from two Greek words: *theos,* meaning God, and *logos,* indicating rational thought. So theology is simply thinking about God and the Hidden World. And that is what we want to do in this book.

Let me explain what I mean by "Christian theology." I have in mind no more than what some people would call the "Christian faith." "Christian theology," as I am using it, carries three basic ideas:

First, I mean that body of truth that Christians use to describe reality. Men and women who are looking for a sensible description of life and its meaning can find it in the Christian faith. It is understandable, intelligible, and true. Not everyone considers it so. I know. But that is what Christians have always claimed and that is what I am trying to set forth in this book.

Second, Christian theology means that body of beliefs Christians have held for two thousand years, the historic faith. The Christian faith is not the peculiar convictions of a Christian believer here and there. Nor is it the exclusive property of a single Christian sect. It is the summation of the teachings of the Bible and the faith of the Christian church throughout the ages.

Third, the Christian faith set forth in this book is my faith. I write not as an analyst; I write as a believer. Christian theology, as I understand it, is not only reasonable and catholic, it is also confessional. This book summarizes my faith. It is what the church has taught me and what I gladly confess.

In underscoring this confessional side of Christian theology, however, I do not want to suggest for a moment that this faith is my private possession in the same way that my attaché case or my desk lamp is mine. My faith is not mine in the sense that I have rights over it. I cannot tamper with it or toss it away. The Christian faith is mine only in the sense that I have accepted it as true. I have received it and have found that it has changed my life.

All this should indicate that this is not intended as another book on "basic Christian doctrine." I am not writing as a theologian to other theologians. My colleagues in theological circles know that I have neither the philosophical preparation nor the personal inclination to write such a book. I have in mind something less ambitious, but more intimate. Throughout these chapters I have tried to imagine a long walk with a friend, new Christian or non-Christian, who has just asked me, "What do you mean by 'the Christian faith'?" So the book—hopefully—is more like an extended personal conversation than the typical introductory course in theology.

That helps to explain the use of "plain language." In attempting to state the Christian faith plainly, I am not attempting to make it easy. I do not believe that is possible. Christianity is not easy to accept, explore, or explain because the gospel rests upon hard facts. The apostle Paul once said that the crucifixion of Jesus Christ was a scandal to the Jews of his day and it was foolishness to the Greeks. Today, men and women who confront the Christian faith for the first time often react in much the same way.

In our talk-show world—where one man's opinion seems to be as good as another's—people try to trace the gospel to the feelings of Christians. It is, they say, the way Christians have come to look at life. Other people, obviously, can look at it differently.

But that is not what Christians claim. They do not believe because they find the Christian faith easy. They believe because they find certain facts *hard*. The facts of the human condition, Jesus Christ's life and death, and the Witness from the Hidden World are simply too compelling to resist. Christians confess that truths—hard facts—have overpowered them and gained control of their thinking and loyalties.

My choice of "plain language" came from the fact that I wanted to present the Christian faith in a straightforward way, a way that people without any formal preparation could understand. There are scores of well-written books about Christian theology for Christians who have spent most of their lives in church. But I wanted a book that set forth the Christian faith for people who knew nothing about theology but wanted an introduction to the Christian faith. Such a person could be a new Christian, or even a person interested in investigating the Christian faith without undue pressure to become a "convert."

To present the Christian faith to such people I chose a simple design. There are many ways to set forth Christianity. At times I think of it as a freshly baked pie. The cook usually slices the pie into pieces so that the only difference in the servings is in size. The filling is the same throughout the pie. It doesn't matter where you begin to remove the pieces from the pie pan.

In the same way, Christian theology is, in one sense, a unified whole. You can slice it many ways and serve it from many directions: the spiritual need of human beings, the character of God, the centrality of Jesus Christ, or the basis of Christian beliefs.

I have chosen to pursue a narrative order. My story has a beginning, a sequence of events, and a rather unpredictable climax. I chose this order because the Bible itself generally follows this sequence. We begin with a self-evident truth: most men and women who try to succeed in life without God encounter frustration, conflict, and emptiness. Why? In spite of what we have heard, do we need faith after all?

We move on to push back the horizons of secular life and ask about the possibility of contact with another world, beyond the sights and sounds of day-to-day existence. Why do we have difficulty contacting that world? What does faith mean? Then we speak of the Ruler of that other realm, and face the fact that he has already made contact with our world. His crucial message, it turns out, was communicated through a first-century Jewish teacher named Jesus Christ. As a result of Jesus' message, death, and life beyond the grave, men and women can now find a new dimension to life, a new outlook upon their week-in-week-out world. People, made alive by contact with the Hidden World, find their hopes and fears and labor dramatically changed because

Jesus came. All who trust in him can look forward to a world beyond this life. Christ's people will some day enter that Hidden World where God is and discover directly and profoundly the meaning of "eternal life."

Summarized in this brief way, the Christian faith sounds like a cosmic myth. But it is no myth. Much of it has already happened, some of it is now unfolding, and the best is yet to come. The point is the Hidden World has contacted our world. Isaiah, the son of Amoz, spoke; Jesus of Nazareth lived; and the People of God endure. The faith is no myth. It is true.

This understanding of reality explains the tone you will find in this book. Since we believe that the Christian faith is true, we hold that other faiths are not fully true. They may be helpful to millions of people. They may be stimulating even to Christians. They may point toward the true faith. But since they are describing reality in another way, they are not true in the same sense that Christianity is true.

We intend no attack on these other faiths, be they non-Christian, counterfeit Christian, or former Christian faiths. To make Christianity itself clear, we have resorted to some comparisons with these other faiths. We have tried to be fair in these comparisons. If we have failed in this attempt, we hope all non-Christians will recognize that our problem is ignorance, not disrespect.

Since I think Christian theology should be catholic (a faith for all times and all people), I have also tried to avoid the disputed emphases of the major denominations in Christianity. I hold some of these teachings myself. I am a Protestant, an evangelical, and a Baptist. I can scarcely hide the fact. But I am also a student of Christian history. I know something of the differences in the catholic faith of all ages and the distinctive beliefs of the various traditions. I have not been able to avoid all references to these differences among Christians, but I have tried to subordinate these differences to the overriding purpose of setting forth the basic beliefs of Christians in all the denominations.

These pages will reveal some of my mentors in this faith. Among them are Augustine, Luther, Pascal, Edward John Carnell, C. S. Lewis, Harry Blamires, J. S. Whale, E. L. Mascall, P. T. Forsyth, Elton Trueblood, John R. W. Stott, and many others. If I have been drawn to an author, I find it is usually due to his unusual insight into the way Christian truth touches the life of man. He has a happy blend of head and heart. He has seen that the faith is more than theology. I hope my readers will find that conviction reflected in these pages as well.

Now that we agree on the direction we want to go, let's get started on this hike.

CHRISTIAN THEOLOGY IN PLAIN LANGUAGE

The Apostles' Creed

The apostles of Jesus did not write The Apostles' Creed. It is the product of gradual development, apparently starting with the "Old Roman Creed" used at Rome late in the second century. The creed, however, has enjoyed wide acceptance in Roman Catholic and Protestant circles.

I believe in God the Father Almighty; Maker of heaven and earth.

And in Jesus Christ his only Son our Lord; who was conceived by the Holy Ghost, born of the Virgin Mary; suffered under Pontius Pilate, was crucified, dead, and buried; he descended into hell; the third day he rose from the dead; he ascended into heaven; and sitteth at the right hand of God the Father Almighty; from thence he shall come to judge the quick and the dead.

I believe in the Holy Ghost; the holy catholic Church; the communion of saints; the forgiveness of sins; the resurrection of the body; and the life everlasting. Amen.

The Nicene Creed *

The Nicene Creed comes closest to serving as a universal Christian creed. It is almost certain that the creed was written for the general council of the church meeting at Constantinople in A.D. 381.

I believe in one God the Father Almighty; Maker of heaven and earth, and of all things visible and invisible.

And in one Lord Jesus Christ, the only-begotten Son of God, begotten of the Father before all worlds, God of God, Light of Light, very God of very God, begotten, not made, being of one substance with the Father; by whom all things were made; who, for us men and for our salvation, came down from heaven, and was incarnate by the Holy Ghost of the virgin Mary, and was made man; and was crucified also for us under Pontius Pilate; he suffered and was buried; and the third day he rose again, according to the Scriptures; and ascended into heaven, and sitteth on the right hand of the Father; and he shall come again, with glory, to judge both the quick and the dead; whose kingdom shall have no end.

And I believe in the Holy Ghost, the Lord and Giver of Life; who proceedeth from the Father [and the Son]; who with the Father and the Son together is worshiped and glorified; who spake by the prophets. And I believe one holy catholic and apostolic church. I acknowledge one baptism for the remission of sins; and I look for the resurrection of the dead, and the life of the world to come. Amen.

---

* The Western addition of the *Filioque* is enclosed in brackets.

1

Lost in the Secular City

Not long ago my wife Mary and I visited a young friend of ours in the hospital. She had just given birth to her first baby. When we arrived at her room, Debbie was holding her tiny son. His little eyes blinked. He yawned just like an adult. His hairline and the shape of his nose reflected his father's rugged face. Little Lance was a living human being; no one could deny it.

During our visit, Debbie said to us, "You know, it was so strange. One minute there were three of us in the delivery room. And the next, there were four." It was her way of describing the wonder of life. Her baby had brought her to the frontier of the Hidden World. What, she asked, is the meaning of life?

The Secular Gospel

The secular world in which Debbie's baby will grow up finds no mystery in his birth, no ultimate purpose in his life, and provides no hope for his hour of death. According to today's secular faith, Lance is a creature of one world. That world has three conditions in which he will live: time, space, and matter. Beyond that, nothing! There is no Hidden World to explain his mother's wonder or to direct his life on Planet Earth. Secularism simply ignores all clues to another world.

Today, in the West as well as in the communist world, the relentless projection of secularism's image of reality makes any clear painting of the Christian faith difficult. Christianity holds that human beings are unique creatures on Planet Earth. They have the potential for contact with another realm of life, a spiritual world of fulfillment and permanence. But the promoters of western secularism say man is simply a highly sexed animal who lives only for the prestige and pleasures of this life.

This secular view of man in North America is part of a strange gospel. The high priests of secularism tell us that we can find personal fulfillment by accumulating more and more things. The steps to success and happiness are rather clear. You go to college; you get a car; you try out several mates and settle on one; then, you buy a house. You work hard—or find the right shortcuts—and you get a significant raise in pay. Then you can move up to a bigger house and buy a better car, always sustained by faith in the promises of the advertisers.

It is a cozy picture. The sun always shines; people always smile. The nearest thing to pain is the arrival of the bills to pay for it all. The only hint that it may end someday is the promise that you will be cushioned by the retirement programs of the Welfare State. That is the sum of life's meaning and purpose: things, pleasure, security, and rest. All in this life.

This secular view of life carries two consequences: First, nothing after death need concern us. If secular men and women think of life after death at all, their thoughts are almost certainly positive. Traditional images of judgment and hell only remain in our society as subjects for laughter. Second, nothing in life need trouble us except the things of this world. God, devils, heaven, and hell play no part in the secular gospel.

Obviously, such a gospel creates an unconscious bias against the Hidden World. No one escapes the incessant propaganda of the secular faith. So we grow up conditioned to scoff at ideas of any reality beyond the dimensions of the natural world.

Will Herberg, the Jewish scholar, once argued that this social brainwashing was a far more important cause of contemporary unbelief than any rational argument from atheism. "What has affected the modern mind," he said, "has not been an array of intellectual arguments, but the unremitting operation of mind-setting attitudes, often hardly noticed, doing their remorseless work by cultural pressures and compulsions." [1]

Life Without Meaning

A number of signs indicate that the proverbial baby has vanished with the bath water. Secular people are left without any ultimate meaning in life. Can material things really satisfy the hunger of the soul? Will constant care of the body fulfill the needs of the spirit?

The question is worth pressing because one of the striking features of today's secular society is moral anarchy—violence, sensuality, dishonesty, crime. I am not suggesting that we ought to encourage religion to get people to behave. My point lies in another direction. If the secular gospel were really what it is touted to be—a guarantee of contentment and happiness—why all the restlessness and rage?

Christians are not alone in pointing out this contemporary bewilderment. The bafflement of modern man's soul is one of the recurring themes in twentieth-century novels and plays. Franz Kafka, D. H. Lawrence, Henry Miller, and Samuel Beckett would never be accused of Christian prejudices, and yet they speak powerfully of the emptiness of men and women without faith.[2]

Similar testimony comes from internationally known psychiatrists. Carl Jung once said, "The central neurosis of our time is emptiness." A supporting diagnosis came from Viktor Frankl, who said that "clinics are crowded with people suffering from a new kind of neurosis, a sense of total and ultimate meaninglessness of life." The frustration comes because man has an "inherent tendency to reach out for meanings to fulfill and values to actualize."

No physician, however, has diagnosed the sickness of the soul without faith any more profoundly than the ancient Hebrew author of Ecclesiastes. He personally sought satisfaction in sensual pleasures, in elaborate houses, and in pursuit of knowledge. And what did he find? He hated life. He discovered that all the good things of this life only lead to disillusionment. Everything, he says, is ". . . meaningless, a chasing after the wind" (1:14).

In literature, stories abound of men who have lost their sense of identity. Some accident, perhaps some blow to the head, has driven them into amnesia and they must wander about the countryside in search of an answer to the maddening question, "Who am I?" Outwardly they look like everyone else, but inwardly they are lost and confused, desperate to know who they are and where they belong.

Early in this century, G. K. Chesterton, the witty British journalist, said that this is the story of every one of us. We have all forgotten who we are. And without some help in finding our true identity we haven't much of an idea what we should be doing.[3]

The Religious Quest

That is the fallacy of the secular faith. It simply does not fit the facts of human existence. It asks us to believe that irrational Nature has managed to produce a race of creatures who ask, "What's behind it all?"

A survey of ancient cultures and contemporary tribes indicates that belief in gods or a God is a common thing. A person who denies completely the Hidden World and insists that there is no purposeful cause behind the universe is a rare creature. Throughout the history of mankind the vast majority of people on Planet Earth have looked for some purpose behind everything. They have sensed that there is more to life than they can see. Someone, or a host of someones, is over us and around us. And since we are surrounded by this greater world, we will have to give an account for the way we have lived on this planet. There must be some life after death.

When a person entertains thoughts like these he is on his way to a religious quest for meaning, because religion is the refusal to believe that the universe can be adequately explained in three-dimensional terms.

The fact that there are several rival sets of beliefs about the unseen world does not mean that all of them are wrong and that one of them cannot be right. If, as Christianity teaches, the Maker has created man in his own image to have fellowship with him, then it isn't surprising if people all over the world and through all the ages have tried to find him.

Once, when the early Christian leader Paul was visiting Athens, he stood before a gathering of the Areopagus and said: "Men of Athens! I see that in every way you are very religious. . . . The God who made the world and everything in it . . . gives all men life and breath and everything else. From one man he made every nation of men, . . . and he determined the times set for them and the exact places where they should live. God did this so that men would seek him and perhaps reach out for him and find him, though he is not far from each one of us" (Acts 17:22–27).

To identify this Hidden World, the German scholar Rudolf Otto coined the term "the numinous." It comes to us, he said, under the dual guise of the terrible and the attractive, awakening in us either awe or delight. The birth of Debbie's baby was obviously a delight. The sudden appearance of a funnel cloud over Kansas can produce a sense of awe. In either case, Christians believe that the Hidden World is real, and they try to understand who is there and what he wants of us.

Such a view of reality rejects secularism and calls for another starting point for the human quest. If secularism proves to be a dead end we have no alternative. We must go back and head in another direction.

In one of his books G. B. Caird, the Oxford professor, tells the story of a yokel who was stopped by a passing traveler and asked, "How can I get to Cambridge from here?" "If I was going to Cambridge," said the yokel, "I wouldn't start from here." [4] Sometimes our starting point is all wrong. So our best move is to look for a new one. Instead of denying the Hidden World, suppose we look for it. Then, where will we find it?

Some world religions counsel us to flee this world of time, space, and matter if we want to find the Hidden World. "There is a state of being beyond this life," they say. "God lives there, and there you must seek him." In other words, we must flee from this world if we want to find the Hidden World.

Remarkably, however, this is not Christianity's counsel. It agrees that the Hidden World exists and God is there, but it also asserts that God himself has visited our world of time, space, and matter. He became one of us. He demonstrated that life in our passing world can be incorporated into his eternal life and that this life can be a genuine prelude for the life to come.

The Image of God

A clue to understanding this intersection of two worlds lies in the nature of man. In some ways man is no different than other species upon the earth. We share time, space, and matter with many other creatures. But in other ways humanity stands out from all the rest. According to the Bible's description of man, he stands out not primarily by what he can do, but by what he is. He is made in "the image of God." We learn something about an artist from his paintings, something about a legislator from his laws, and something about a parent from his children. We likewise discover something about God in man.

Christians have often debated the meaning of that "image." It is probably not limited to a single characteristic, but at the heart of its meaning is the special capacity to live in a personal relationship with God.

In the biblical story of man's creation we read that Adam walked and talked with God. God and man were able to communicate personally with one another. On one hand, man could communicate with God: he could worship him and thank him. And on the other hand, God could speak to man. He could explain his purposes and plans for him. The "image of God" in man, then, means the power to love and serve his Maker and his fellows.

Today, we know that men and women do not do this well or often. Something has apparently gone wrong with the original plan. And if a thing fails in its essential purpose, its very existence is endangered. A fire that does not burn is not a fire. Man, however, reveals his restlessness about the failure.

"Do fish complain of the sea for being wet?" C. S. Lewis, the Cambridge University scholar, once asked. "Or if they did, would the fact not strongly suggest that they had not always been, or would not always be, purely aquatic creatures? If you are really a product of a material universe, how is it that you don't feel at home there?" Man's hunger, said Lewis, does not prove that he will be fed. He may starve, but surely his hunger says that his body needs food and that it comes from a world where the stuff exists.[5]

Christians find reflections of this smudged image of God in several human characteristics. Man, for example, has a sense of obligation. He seems to think it matters how he lives. Somewhere, people have gotten the idea that certain attitudes and actions are right and others are wrong. They even teach these ideas to their children. And the strangest thing is that so many people can give no rational explanation for these ideas. They just know that a person should not harm those who are kindest to him, or steal an old lady's last few dollars, or beat children, or any of the number of other things that contradict ideas of justice, decency, and fair play.

We even make laws to try to keep others from violating these standards. Every now and then you hear someone say, "You can't legislate morality." But that is a ridiculous statement. Nearly all legislation is aimed at protecting moral standards. They are basic to human existence.

Even when man is acting most like an animal, he knows that he is a special creature. Think of the contrasts with our furry friends. No one thinks of stopping an alley cat from clawing another one by saying, "Hey, take it easy!" But a man, who through careless driving maims another person, feels guilty. He knows what he did is not what he should have done.

Of course, people do break these standards, and they will try to excuse themselves or argue that the rule they broke was not all that important. But as soon as someone else wrongs them, they appeal to the same moral standards, protesting that the action against them was wrong or unfair. The atheistic scientist will still deny another man's right to steal his research.

Where did man get this sense of obligation? Are we to believe that some body fluid produces it? Or is it a reflection of the One who created man? Isn't that what we should expect? If people are in any way the likeness of their Creator, their moral sense should reflect it. That, at any rate, is what the Bible suggests. It says when people without a written moral code—"Gentiles"—"do by nature things required by the law . . . they show that the requirements of the law are written on their hearts" (Rom. 2:14–15).

Or consider another human trait, a kind of spiritual touch with nature. Why, for example, are human beings moved by unusual experiences? We can analyze music in terms of vibrations and acoustics, but we cannot explain its effect on the human soul. We experience more than some scientific reaction when we watch crashing waves, or smell the smoke of pine logs burning, or feel the breeze that wafts through the oak leaves.

"It is," wrote the Bible translator J. B. Phillips, "as though there was another dimension. . . . We may well begin to suspect that this physical world is in fact shot through and through with spiritual realities." [6] Humans seem to sense that spiritual dimension.

Christians hold that these special human qualities are clues to life's purpose, memories of a kingdom long gone. "Who is unhappy at not being a king," Blaise Pascal, the seventeenth-century genius, once asked, "except a deposed king? All of these miseries of man prove man's greatness. They are the miseries of a deposed king." His point was well taken. People are born into royalty but they have been expelled from the kingdom. They are children of God but have lost contact with their Father.

We can understand, then, why little Lance's birth was for Debbie more than a routine experience. It was a personal pointer to the Hidden World, and the heavenly Father's house.

2

We Are Not Alone

Out of the depths of his own personal agony Job, an ancient Near Eastern patriarch, sobbed,

> If only I knew where to find him;
>   if only I could go to his dwelling!
> I would state my case before him
>   and fill my mouth with arguments.
> I would find out what he would answer me,
>   and consider what he would say.
>   (Job 23:3–5)

This ancient tragedy, the story of Job's losses of property, health, and family is a striking reminder of the inadequacies of our human horizons for a satisfying view of life and its sorrows. There is something profoundly Christian about Job's discovery that human wisdom alone offers no adequate explanation of life's meaning. In one sense men are never prepared to hear from the Hidden World until they have discovered secularism's silence. "If only I knew where to find God!"

Man, it seems, shares a universal concern: How can I contact reality? Where can I find God?

The earth teems with religions, each of them offering some explanation of man's quest for life's meaning. We can reduce this number, however, to three basic views: atheism, pantheism, and theism.

31

Basic Religious Views

The first view, atheism, says no God exists. Man's belief in God is a figment of the human imagination. Man, says the atheist, invented the term *God* to explain those mysteries in life that he could not fathom.

Bertrand Russell, the British philosopher, once intoned the atheist's creed in his own unique style. An atheist, he confessed, believes "that man is the product of causes which had no prevision of the end they were achieving; that his origin, his growth, his hopes and fears, his loves and beliefs, are but the outcome of accidental collocations of atoms; that no fire, no heroism, no intensity of thought or feeling, can preserve an individual life beyond the grave; that all the labor of the ages, all the devotion, all the inspiration, all the noonday brightness of human genius, are destined to extinction in the vast death of the solar system." [1]

Such a creed needs no word from God. There is no God to speak. So how does man find reality?

Many atheists accept the religion of humanism. The humanist finds nothing in the universe to worship; he calls instead for a special reverence for Man. (And he insists on the capitalization of the term.) He believes that Man can invest his passing existence with meaning if he will rely upon the powers of reason, including science and education, to create and attain self-improvement and social progress for mankind.

For almost 300 years human reason has reigned in the Western world, as David Hume, the eighteenth-century philosopher, once said, "prescribing laws and imposing maxims, with an absolute sway." In intellectualized religions, such as humanism, this "god" judges truth and life itself by the laws of logical consistency. Reality must bow before the throne of the human mind.

As even Hume himself acknowledged, however, reason alone can never demonstrate its right to rule. Men and women are merely finite beings. Their grasp of reality is too small. They will never generate sufficient wisdom to answer the questions of the universe or to understand reality's fullness.

The second fundamental view of reality is pantheism. Unlike atheism which finds God nowhere, pantheism finds God everywhere. Its distinctive belief is summed up in its name, from two Greek words. *Pan* means all and *theos* means God. So to the pantheist "God is all and all is God." In other words, he identifies God with the universe and the universe with God. Pantheists, therefore, do not believe in a God who has an existence apart from the world and who chose to create the universe by his own powerful Word.

One primitive form of pantheism, accepted today by 100 million people in Africa, Asia, and South America, is animism. An animist believes that the natural world is filled and "animated" by unseen forces called spirits or gods. Like their ancestors before them, animists sense intuitively powers above and within them and their world.

Their fathers were so often subject to the forces of nature—wind and fire and rain—that they often personified and deified these powers. When rains flooded their crops, the animists took their misfortune as the angry voice of the rain god. The best course seemed to lie in appeasing his wrath. So they brought to the angry spirit an offering or a sacrifice. When rains fell gently, bringing a welcome harvest, animists believed that the rain god had shown his favor and that they should respond with thanksgiving.

This line of thinking filled pantheons in ancient Greece and groves in Canaan. But these gods do not fully answer man's dilemma. They may address the powers of nature—they may even give the worshiper a sense of oneness with the universe—but they do not give life meaning. They lack a reference point outside the painful passage of time. They do not satisfy Job's search for a word of comfort from a God out there who can hear his complaint.

Think of the pantheist's life as a ship at sea. On board it is impossible to tell how fast the ship is moving by looking either at the surging water or at the furniture on the deck. Moving with the tide the ship seems to cut through the ocean effortlessly, while in fact it is speeding through the waves. When sailing against the current the opposite is true. The waters move swiftly by but the ship makes little progress. It is impossible to know the ship's actual speed without some fixed point, some North Star, to serve as a point of reference.

Spiritual reality is the same. As long as we search inside ourselves or in the world about us, we will never find the answers to our questions about meaning. We need some fixed point outside our world.

Christians—and others who hold the third view of reality, theism—believe that reality's North Star is a message from the Hidden World. The Creator of heaven and earth has not left man to die in Russell's cosmic silence. He has spoken to us. He has chosen to disclose his purpose to man. Job's question, then, is not the appropriate one to ask. It is not, "How can we find God?" It is rather, "How has God revealed himself to us?"

When Christians consider the ways God speaks to us, they recognize two types of revelation: one through his world and the other through his Word. They call them general revelation and special revelation. The two differ in their audiences and in their aims.

General revelation is given to all people of all times. It is the fingerprint of God left on the works of creation. Special revelation is given to specific people at specific times. It is a message from God explaining his purpose in a special segment of history. General revelation indicates that God exists but that man refuses to honor him as a generous Creator. Special revelation does more. It discloses God's character, his plans for mankind, and his saving works. It calls men and women to repentance and faith in God.

"All men have the general knowledge," Martin Luther, the Protestant reformer, once said. "But what God thinks of us, what he wants to give and do to deliver us from sin and death and to save us—this men do not know. Thus it can happen that someone's face may be familiar to me but I do not really know him, because I do not know what he has in his mind. So it is that men know naturally that there is a God, but they do not know what he wants and what he does not want." [2]

God's Familiar Face

We find God's general revelation in his creation. The natural order—the world of sights and smells and sounds—is filled with hints and clues of the presence and power of God: the lightning's flash, the spider's web, the galaxy's order. These and countless other impressions from the universe are whispers of the God who made them all. The ancient Hebrews sang of this wonder:

> The heavens declare the glory of God;
> the skies proclaim the work of his hands.
> (Ps. 19:1)

Paul, the early Christian evangelist, agreed. Since the creation of the world, he said, "God's invisible qualities—his eternal power and divine nature—have been clearly seen." Man detects these qualities in the things God has made (Rom. 1:20).

The tribesmen of Ecuador and Indonesia are not entirely misled in fearing the spirits of the forests and streams. The visible world does veil an invisible one. Their sin, like our own, lies in worshiping and serving created things rather than the Creator. The brush strokes of nature are designed to introduce us to the Artist. He set us in the world of wonders, not to make us idolaters, but to make us thankful.

Of all the things that God has made none carries his image quite like man. The power of reason, by which man questions God's existence, is itself a sign of God's handiwork. As we have said, reason alone is ill equipped to sit in judgment of God's truth. That is impossible. No human mind is capable of that. But our ability to think at all is a reflection of God's character. He is no irrational force. He is the Source of all reason. If that were not so we could never understand his self-disclosure.

Without reason, we have no basis for insisting that one faith is any better or any worse than another. All talk of God or religion would be so much meaningless babbling. But if God is rational, then we may expect his message to us to be reasonable.

In the end, the general revelation from God discloses man's

potential; it does not solve his problem. Man knows enough to confess that he does not know. This general revelation shows that people have longings they cannot satisfy because they are made for a homeland they have fled. "Our lifelong nostalgia," C. S. Lewis once said, "to be on the inside of some door which we have always seen from the outside, is no mere neurotic fancy, but the truest index of our real situation." [3]

The Authority of the Bible

The Christian faith holds that God has chosen to speak to man not only through creation, but through a special stream of human history recorded in the Bible. We call this special revelation because it carries a special message from God to the ancient people of Israel and to their spiritual heirs in the Christian church.

That claim, I know, sparks a powder keg of questions: How can the eternal God be revealed in and through human history? How can time carry the message of eternity? God by common understanding is universal and history is the story of particulars. The very expression "historical revelation" borders on the absurd.

Christians have never denied the difficulty. The apostle Paul once said, "We preach Christ crucified . . . unto the Greeks foolishness" (1 Cor. 1:23, KJV). Men would never have dreamed of such a story. It is only because it actually happened that Christians ever got the idea of preaching it.

In other words, the inscrutable God who inhabits eternity has himself bridged the chasm into time. He decided to communicate with men by the way men can understand, through human history. The omnipresent and eternal God made himself known in the temporal process. One special segment of history became his channel of communication and reached a climax in his ultimate message: "The Word became flesh and lived for a while among us" (John 1:14)—perhaps the most astonishing statement in the whole Bible.

When the Bible uses the expression the "Word of God" it intends what Christians call God's *revelation*, the words or actions of God through which he makes himself known to man.

We read that by his Word, God created the heavens and the earth. "By the word of the Lord were the heavens made, their starry host by the breath of his mouth" (Ps. 33:6). By his Word God also spoke to the Hebrew prophets. Their constant claim was "the Word of the Lord came unto me." Finally, in the last days he spoke through Jesus Christ, his special Son (Heb. 1:1–2). By announcing this revelation of God, Christians make spiritual life available to those who believe the message. Men and women find genuine faith in the way they hear the Word and gain new life by its power (Rom. 10:17).

According to the Bible, the Word of God—this lively revelation from God—is both an event within human history and an explanation of its meaning. Put another way, the Word is both an act of God and an utterance of God. For example, it is both the exodus of Israel from Egypt and the Law delivered at Mount Sinai. It conveys an element of power along with an element of truth. The Word has the unique ability to bring a person face to face with the Living God and to hold him accountable for his life before God.

We call this power to demand men's obedience divine *authority.* In ordinary life we settle disputes by appealing to an authority. It may be a book of law, a medical journal, or a flight schedule. In any case, an authority carries the power to settle an issue. So in matters about God and his relationships with men, the authority is the Word of God.

Christians have always believed that the Scriptures—first the Old Testament, then the addition of the New Testament—share in this authority. They are more than a mere record of the Word of God. They are the Word of God in the sense that they also convey the message of God's acts, and they act upon the souls of men and call for a response to God. Scholars cannot extract somehow the great truths from the history of Israel or from Jesus' teaching to create general religious principles for humanity, later discarding the biblical events as myths. Truth is in the biblical story, and power is in its telling. That is why the Bible sets the standard for beliefs in Christianity.

Obviously, men and women can read the Bible simply as ancient

Hebrew literature. They do it all the time. But when Christians speak of the Bible as the Word of God they are talking about what C. S. Lewis once called "getting the focus right." It is possible, he said, for a person to contend that a poem is nothing but black marks on white paper. And such an argument might be convincing before an audience that could not read. You can examine the print under a microscope or analyze the paper and ink but you will never find something behind this sort of analysis that you could call "a poem." Those who can read, however, will continue to insist that poems exist.[4]

One of the terms Christians use to describe this special focus of the Bible is *inspiration.* It is a well worn word in English. A soccer team, we say, played an inspired game against a stronger opponent. Or we might try to explain to a friend the inspiration we felt during the playing of Tchaikovsky's *1812 Overture.* The word used in this context means an exalting or elevating state. No doubt the biblical prophets and apostles also had these inspired moments.

Christians, however, mean more than that in speaking of the Bible's inspiration. They mean that the Bible came to men as a result of God's initiative, not man's. That, at any rate, is what the Bible often says about the writings of the prophets and apostles.

The idea, though not the word, appears in a rather well-known passage in 2 Timothy 3:16. It says Scripture was "breathed of God," a Hebrew way of saying that something was produced by the power or energy of God.

Another passage—2 Peter 1:20–21—uses a different image for God's activity. It says the prophets of God were "carried along" like a ship propelled by winds filling its sails. Inspiration, then, stands for all the activities of God in selecting, moving, and informing the prophets of the Old Testament and the apostles of the New in the course of their writing the Scriptures.

This activity of God seldom overwhelmed the authors. They were not carried away into a mystical world of heavenly truths. They retained their individuality, with styles and perspectives uniquely their own. Some were scholars; others were peasants.

Some were rural; others were urban. Each brought his own vocabulary, temperament, and experience to his special role in communicating the Word.

As a consequence, Christians hold that the Bible is both a divine and a human Book. It communicates the Word of God, yet it calls for study like any other piece of literature. It is both the Word of God and the words of men. It demands submission and faith, but simultaneously requires study and interpretation.

If God does speak in Scripture, what language does he use? There is a story about an elderly lady who took up Hebrew in her advanced years because she wanted to be able to greet her Maker in his native tongue. That, I fear, is taking a biblical figure of speech to a humorous extreme.

The Bible often speaks of the spiritual realities of the Hidden World. To make these realms intelligible to us it employs symbolic or metaphorical language. That poses a troublesome problem for many people. If we take these expressions literally, as the elderly lady did, they will mislead us. We use no scales to measure the weight of an argument and no mathematics to calculate the height of a lofty ideal. We never get a suntan from the glow of a sunny disposition or the illumination of a brilliant scholar. In day-to-day conversation we seem to manage metaphors quite well. Why should we have so much trouble understanding the Bible?

Some people, when they recognize a biblical metaphor, tend to dilute the image to some vapid moralism. They have the good sense to recognize that hell "fire" is a metaphor, but they unwisely conclude that it means nothing more serious than inward remorse, something we often experience this side of the grave. Or they rightly think that the apostle spoke metaphorically when he said Christians are "raised to walk in newness of life," but they misunderstand him completely if they think he meant the Christian faith consists of nothing more than a respectable life in acceptable society.

This type of interpretation is so common that it creates a distinct impression that some people do not have as much trouble with biblical metaphors as with biblical miracles. If that is true, these people will never understand the Bible or Christianity. If you subtract the miraculous elements from the Hindu's pantheism, all the essential beliefs remain. The same is obviously true of humanism. But Christianity without miracles is not Christianity. It is something else.

Job came to see that. At one point in his depression he looked for God in order to state his case. When he finally encountered the Lord, he learned that in the presence of God man does not fill his mouth with words, but with wonder.

3

The Exodus and the Entrance

In the year A.D. 303, the Roman Emperor Diocletian issued a decree which he hoped would extinguish the spreading flames of Christianity. One of his primary objectives was the seizure and destruction of the Christian Scriptures.

Later that year, officials enforced the decree in North Africa. One of the targets was Felix, Bishop of Tibjuca, a village near Carthage. The mayor of the town ordered Felix to hand over his Scriptures. Though some judges were willing to accept scraps of parchment, Felix refused to surrender the Word of God at the insistence of mere men. Resolutely, he resisted compromise.

Roman authorities finally shipped Felix to Italy where he paid for his stubbornness with his life. On August 30, as the record puts it, "with pious obstinacy," he laid down his life rather than surrender his Gospels.[1]

In our day when the Bible is so readily available we may find Felix's dogged determination mystifying. It does highlight, however, a fact of central importance for understanding the Christian faith: Christianity is inextricably linked to the Bible. All its basic affirmations arise from the story of the ancient people of Israel and their most controversial offshoot, the Jesus movement. We may justifiably ask, then, what is the Bible all about?

At first glance the Bible is a strange sort of Book. It contains sixty-six smaller books, written by approximately forty authors over a period of sixteen hundred years. The first thirty-nine books, called the Old Testament, were originally Jewish Scriptures and were written mostly in Hebrew. The twenty-seven books called the New Testament were written later by Christians in Greek.

The Old Testament is often divided into the Law (the first five books), the Prophets, and the Writings, which include the popular Psalms and Proverbs. The New Testament can be divided into the Gospels (four of them) and the Epistles (letters). The Acts of the Apostles serves as a historical bridge from the Gospels to the Epistles. The last book, Revelation, provides a unique climax to the whole collection.

The thread running through the sixty-six books is the story of man's rebellion against God, his Creator, and God's merciful acts seeking man's repentance and faith. The story is no myth. It really happened. That is one reason we say Christianity is a historical religion. God's message about himself and his reconciliation of man is an unfolding history of a nation called Israel and a Person called Jesus. The Christian faith cannot be divorced from this biblical story.

Biblical history, however, is not identical with our modern view of history. A modern historian is supposed to give an objective account of the facts of his era. But biblical history is interpreted history. Biblical authors have a point of view. They share a testimony as well as tell a story.

The authors were selective, therefore, in their choice of material. Rather than focus on the movements of the mighty ancient empires—Assyria, Babylon, Persia, Egypt, Greece, and Rome—they included these only as they impinged on the relatively inconsequential Israelite communities in Palestine. The Bible is not concerned with the wisdom, wealth, or might of this world, but with the salvation provided by God.

The Start of the Story

The story begins with time itself: "In the beginning God created the heavens and the earth." On the sixth day of creation the

Lord crowned his work by fashioning man "in his own image." When God checked on his handiwork, he saw that it was very good—but not for long. Only three chapters from the beginning man stumbled into moral ruin. The rest of the Bible is the story of his rescue.

After the initial sin of the original pair, Adam and Eve, mankind plunged into the grossest immorality. God even regretted that he had made man, so he decided to destroy the earth by a flood. With an eye on the future, however, he arranged for a single surviving household—Noah and his family.

Even this dreadful judgment failed to cure man of his depravity. Noah's descendants took the same path as Adam. In their pride they refused to accept God as God and to worship him.

As a result, somewhere around 2000 B.C., God decided to implement a new strategy in his dealings with men. He turned to a specific people who became his new beachhead in the world.

A nation began with a single man, Abraham. While living in Ur of the Chaldees (ancient Mesopotamia and modern Iraq), Abraham heard God's call: "Leave your country, your people and your father's household and go to the land I will show you." Then God offered Abraham a promise. "I will make you into a great nation and I will bless you . . . I will bless those who bless you, and whoever curses you I will curse; and all peoples on earth will be blessed through you" (Gen. 12:1–3). The remainder of the Bible is the unfolding of this promise, called the *covenant*.

Abraham passed on this promise to his son, Isaac, born to Abraham and Sarah when they were beyond their childbearing years. Isaac repeated the promise to his son Jacob, whose name was also Israel. Finally, Jacob passed the promise to his twelve sons, the heads of the twelve tribes of Israel.

Through the treachery of his brothers, Joseph, one of Jacob's sons, was sold into slavery in Egypt. But, as Joseph himself put it, what his brothers intended for evil, God intended for good. Joseph the slave became Joseph the Vice-Pharaoh, his authority second only to the power of the Pharaoh (or king) of Egypt.

When a famine struck Canaan, Jacob and his family moved to Egypt where Joseph provided all their needs. For 430 years Israel's descendants flourished and multiplied there.

Joseph probably came to power during the reign of the Hyksos rulers (about 1700 B.C.), the foreign "shepherd kings" who ruled between Egyptian dynasties. These favorable years ended, however, when "a new king arose over Egypt who did not know Joseph" (Exod. 1:8, NASB). This new Pharaoh, perhaps Rameses II, conscripted the Hebrews into labor camps and stone quarries. And the people of Israel cried out to God for deliverance; "and God heard their groaning, and God remembered his covenant with Abraham . . ." (Exod. 2:24, RSV).

Deliverance came from an unexpected source, Pharaoh's own palace. After training in the royal courts and lonely experiences in the Sinai wilderness, Moses was ready to fulfill his destiny. He heard the call from the Lord and delivered God's message to Pharaoh: "Let my people go." Pharaoh's determined resistance provoked God to send a series of plagues, the last one killing all of the firstborn sons in Egypt except those of the Hebrews. Jews still celebrate the event in the Passover holiday. Pharaoh's resistance finally crumbled. He let the people go.

The Israelites were hardly on the road when Pharaoh reverted to his former stubbornness and pursued the bedraggled band of ex-slaves. With the sea before them and approaching Egyptian troops behind, the Israelites watched as Moses stretched out his staff and the sea parted.

We do not know the exact location of the "Red Sea"—as the King James Bible translated it—or the "Sea of Reeds"—as the Hebrew Bible says. But we do know that the water was deep enough to drown a battalion of Egyptian soldiers, and to splash the Exodus forever across Hebrew memory.

The Covenant at Sinai

The ragged multitude of grumbling Israelites eventually reached the foot of Mount Sinai, where Moses had met God at a burning bush years before. Here God gave Israel three special gifts: the renewed covenant, a moral law, and an atoning sacrifice.

The covenant came first. "You have seen what I did to the Egyptians," God told Israel, "and how I bore you on eagles' wings and brought you to myself. Now, therefore, if you will obey my voice and keep my covenant, you shall be my own possession among all peoples" (Exod. 19:4–5, RSV). The people happily accepted God's covenant.

Keeping this covenant meant obeying God's moral law. Its essence was the Ten Commandments, which gave Israel the essentials for maintaining a right relationship with God and with men.

But what if the people broke the moral law? That was the purpose of the sacrificial system and the ceremonial law. Every dramatic action of the system carried some message and looked forward to that final, once-for-all sacrifice of the perfect Lamb that God would one day offer.

With the law in hand, the chosen people headed for their promised land. When they reached the border of Palestine, however, they halted in faithless fear. The inhabitants of the land seemed like giants to them. Their unbelief provoked the Lord. He condemned his people to wandering in the wilderness until every adult of that generation perished. Only after forty years, under the leadership of Joshua, did the people of promise enter the land of promise.

Joshua's first responsibility as leader of the Israelites was the conquest of the local inhabitants, the Canaanites. After a series of military victories, Joshua parceled out the land to the twelve tribes of Israel. But he failed to subdue the local populations. As a result, the Canaanites persisted as a constant source of political and religious irritation.

The Book of Judges illustrates this repeatedly. Time and again the Israelites succumbed to the worship of Baal and Ashtaroth, the local Canaanite fertility gods. The Lord would respond by allowing an oppressor to gain the upper hand over one of the tribes. When the people called on the Lord for deliverance, he sent a judge, a military leader, who broke the bonds of the oppressor.

After 200 years of these ups and downs, and especially the

defeat at the hands of the Philistines, the Israelites had had enough. They cried out for a king, "that we also may be like all the nations" (1 Sam. 8:20, RSV).

The Age of Kings (1050–586 B.C.)

God complied with the Israelites' request and gave them a king. They chose Saul, the strongest, handsomest man in Israel. Though Saul was somewhat successful in his military exploits, he was not always content to obey the Lord. Three times he specifically disregarded direct commands of God. His downfall began when a young shepherd boy named David won the praise of Israel by defeating the Philistine hero, Goliath. Saul was wild with jealousy and spent his last years as king haplessly hounding David, the anointed heir to his throne.

Whereas Saul was a king by popular choice, David was a king by God's choice. Under David's dynamic leadership, Israel subdued her enemies and extended her borders: from the "River of Egypt" (Egypt's frontier wadi extending into the Sinai) to the River Euphrates in Mesopotamia.

David was more than an ancient warlord. He was also an artist—a musician in Saul's court. He had a sensitive spirit, and he was generous with his enemies and loyal to his friends. Above all, he was devoted to the Lord. Aside from his tragic sin against Bathsheba and Uriah, his life was marked by exceptional piety. The Psalms he wrote reveal an unsurpassed depth of spirituality.

As he had with Moses, God renewed his covenant with David. But this time he added a new note: the permanence of the Davidic throne. "Your house and your kingdom shall be made sure for ever before me" (2 Sam. 7:16, RSV). This became the keynote of Israel's hope for the next 400 years. God would sustain the Davidic line until the ultimate triumph of Messiah, the special leader in Israel's future.

David was succeeded by his son, Solomon. Gifted with unusual wisdom, Solomon brought Israel to a zenith of economic prosperity, peace, and strength. Unfortunately he achieved much of his success by conscripted labor. Solomon's major weakness, however, was women. In defiance of the Lord's prohibition of inter-marriage, he kept a harem of foreign princesses, and they "turned his heart after their gods."

Rehoboam, Solomon's son, inherited his father's troubles as well as his throne. The men of the north who had groaned under Solomon's oppressive measures, demanded a reprieve from Reho-boam. The king replied with threats of a heavier yoke for the necks of such grumblers. He succeeded in provoking the ten northern tribes into seceding from the Davidic dynasty. After 120 years, the kingdom of Israel was irreparably split. Only the tribes of Judah and Benjamin remained loyal to the throne estab-lished by God's covenant.

A former government official named Jeroboam assumed the leadership of the northern kingdom, sometimes called Israel, sometimes called Ephraim. He faced problems immediately. The temple that Solomon had built was in Jerusalem, Rehoboam's capital. If Jeroboam's subjects made pilgrimages there, he was bound to lose their loyalty. So he built two alternative sanctuaries, in which he installed altars resting on golden calves: one in Dan, the other in Bethel.

This relieved his political problem but insured his infamy in the annals of Israel's history. The pro-Davidic author of the books of Kings makes this clear. Without exception, the kings of the north "did evil in the eyes of the Lord." Often the author gets specific by charging that they "followed in the sins of Jeroboam which he caused Israel to commit."

The period of the divided kingdom was a time of political intrigue, military conflicts, and religious apostasy. The Lord fi-nally sent judgment on Israel in the form of the powerful Assyri-ans. In 722 B.C. Shalmaneser V besieged and destroyed Samaria and deported 27,000 inhabitants of the nation (2 Kings 17:3–6). The ten tribes were assimilated into native populations.

The southern kingdom, called Judah, was a different story, in part. Though the dynasty of David continued, his descendants did not inherit his devotion. The authors of Kings and Chronicles tell us that most "did evil in the eyes of the Lord" by tolerating religious syncretism. Despite the efforts of occasional reformers, such as Hezekiah and Josiah, Judah also provoked the Lord. Judgment came in the form of Nebuchadnezzar, King of Babylon, who razed Jerusalem in 586 B.C.

What happened to God's promise to David that his throne would never end? Had God abandoned his people and his promise? During these years of crisis, prophets appeared in Judah offering an answer to that question. Isaiah, for example, preached that all nations—even the mighty Assyrian Empire—were merely tools of God's plan for the final salvation of mankind. Judah's suffering would produce "a remnant of Israel" that would return to their homeland and preside over a coming age of righteousness and peace.

Though the northern kingdom was entirely lost, Judah suffered exile for only seventy years. When Cyrus of Persia conquered Babylon, he allowed the Jews to return and rebuild their city and their temple. This they did under the leadership of Zerubbabel (who rebuilt the temple), Ezra (who brought the people back to the Law), and Nehemiah (who rebuilt the walls of Jerusalem). Here, under the prophetic ministries of Haggai, Zechariah, and Malachi, the Old Testament concludes.

Intertestamental Times

Though most Bibles simply add the New Testament to the prophecies of the Old, nearly 400 years of history unfolded between Malachi and Matthew. We may view this period as God's preparation of the world for the coming of the Messiah, Jesus of Nazareth.

At the end of the Old Testament Judah was a tiny vassal state of the mighty Persian Empire. It remained so until 333 B.C., when Alexander the Great of Macedonia (northern Greece), subdued Persia and assumed authority over the Jews. Upon Alexander's death, his power passed to four of his generals. The Jews, heirs of ancient Israel, fell under the jurisdiction of Ptolemy, whose state was centered in Alexandria, Egypt.

In a sense, Alexander's conquests prepared the world for the Christian faith. First, Greek philosophy spread into conquered lands. Greek ideas of monotheism, immortality, and morality formed a point of contact between Christianity and the pagan world.

Second, the Greek language appeared as the common trade language in all the Mediterranean world and remained so for nearly 500 years. This enabled people like the apostle Paul to preach in a single language over a broad geographical area. During the Ptolemaic period, scholars translated the Old Testament into Greek (the Septuagint) and thus made the Bible available to hosts of new readers.

In 198 B.C. the Seleucids, the Syrian segment of Alexander's empire, annexed Palestine. Within a generation the Syrian king, Antiochus Epiphanes, instituted a policy of oppression against the Jews and outlawed their religion. When soldiers attempted to force Mattathias, the high priest, to sacrifice to pagan gods, he and his family instigated a rebellion. By means of guerilla warfare, the so-called "Maccabean revolt" successfully shed the shackles of the Seleucids and established the free state of Israel.

Freedom, however, was short lived. The Maccabean rulers fell into the same trap as their forefathers. Corruption helped to guarantee their eventual fall in 63 B.C. at the hands of the Romans. Twenty-three years later the Roman senate passed the scepter to Herod the Great, "King of the Jews" who ruled the land when Jesus was born in Bethlehem.

Jesus of Nazareth

The story of Jesus, his disciples, and the early development of Christianity is recorded in the pages of the New Testament. Two of the Gospels—Matthew and Luke—attribute the birth of Jesus to an act of God. The Lord spoke to a Jewish peasant girl, Mary, and her husband-to-be named Joseph. He told them that by the power of the Holy Spirit she would give birth to a son and they were to name him "Yeshua" (Jesus), which in Hebrew means "the Lord saves." According to the Gospels these descendants of David did just as they were told. And God miraculously gave them a son.

Beyond these birth narratives of Matthew and Luke, we know almost nothing about Jesus' early years. When Jesus was nearly thirty, however, his cousin, John, began to preach in the Judean wilderness and baptize in the Jordan River. He told the crowds who came to hear him that he was a herald for a leader yet to come.

Jesus' own baptism by John proved to be a profound spiritual experience. Immediately afterward, he suffered satanic assaults for forty days in the wilderness, and then launched his three-year mission in Israel. The first year was marked by relative obscurity, the second by popularity, and the third by adversity.

During the first year Jesus concentrated on two objectives: reaching out to numbers of people and gathering a small band of disciples: Peter, Matthew, John, the son of Zebedee, and others. After a few months in the south, Jesus concentrated on the villages of Galilee, away from official Judaism in Jerusalem.

As his reputation spread the second year, he gave himself to wider circles of preaching, teaching, and working miracles. The theme of his message was the "gospel of the kingdom." The true kingdom, he said, was the personal reign of God in human lives, and he had come to inaugurate that rule. The arrival of the kingdom was the fulfillment of the Old Testament hope. But in order to "receive," "enter," or "inherit" the kingdom men must repent and believe, humbly accepting its privileges and submitting to its demands like little children.

In teaching his disciples Jesus explained what it meant to live as people of the kingdom. Perhaps the best example of the new law of the kingdom appears in his Sermon on the Mount. A disciple's righteousness, he said, is unlike the religions of the Pharisees and the pagans. The Jewish people called Pharisees practiced a strict faith that often slipped into hypocrisy. On the other hand, the pagans, who lived without the guidance of the Law, used religion as an excuse for selfish gratification. Righteousness, Jesus told his disciples, must spring from a new heart.

Jesus' miracles were themselves a type of teaching. Most of them were healings used as signs of God's kingdom and Jesus' authority. The impact of these "signs and wonders" carried Jesus to the heights of his popularity when he fed 5000 Passover pilgrims. The crowd was so elated that they tried to make Jesus king. Jesus, however, was convinced that the people totally misunderstood his mission. He withdrew quietly to more isolated regions to inform his close friends about his true purpose.

Jesus' popularity with the people provoked the Jewish authorities to jealousy and led to the last phase of his public ministry: adversity. Herod Antipas, ruler of Galilee, feared that Jesus might be the Messiah whom John the Baptist had predicted. So with the help of some of the Pharisees, he laid plans to arrest Jesus and kill him. Jesus learned of the plot however, and fled to Judea with his disciples.

After several months of preaching, Jesus made his final pilgrimage to Jerusalem for Passover. Accompanied by a large procession, he entered the Temple where he drove out the peddlers of sacrificial animals. On the eve of Passover Jesus and his twelve disciples celebrated their last meal together. Late that night, soldiers sent by the high priest arrested Jesus.

Before the Sanhedrin, the Jewish high court, Jesus was convicted of blasphemy. Since the Sanhedrin had no authority to execute him, they rushed him to the Roman governor, Pontius Pilate, who sentenced him to death by crucifixion. Soldiers carried out the order: a painful death on the cross.

The Birth of Christianity

Within days rumors were circulating in Jerusalem that Jesus was no longer dead. He had risen from the grave. The disciples regathered and two months later, empowered by a new Spirit, they began preaching in Jerusalem's synagogues that Jesus was the promised Messiah. God had confirmed it by raising him from the dead. Forgiveness of sins and the power of the Spirit, they said, were available to anyone who repented and accepted Jesus as Lord.

Among the new believers were some who spoke Greek. They were called Hellenists. Their increasing numbers alarmed the Jewish authorities. One Christian leader named Stephen was stoned to death by an angry mob after he dared to challenge Jewish traditions. The instigator of this assault was a Pharisee, Paul of Tarsus. Intent on destroying this new heresy, Paul set out for Damascus. But on the way he had a vivid encounter with the resurrected Jesus, which transformed him into a zealous Christian.

Through Paul's tireless missionary efforts, Christianity spread from its Jewish roots in Judea into Gentile cities from Antioch in Syria to the imperial capital, Rome. When he was unable to visit the fledgling churches, Paul wrote letters to encourage or instruct them. In most cities he faced persecution from pagans or from his fellow Jews. Upon his return from a third missionary journey Jewish leaders secured his imprisonment in Jerusalem. From there Roman authorities moved him to Caesarea, a coastal town, and later to Rome to await trial. He died during Nero's persecution of Christians, but left his mark upon Christianity through the theology strikingly expressed in his letters.

This is the story that ties together the sixty-six books of the Bible and discloses the epochal realities of the Christian faith.

4

The Ranks of the Resistance

During World War II Japanese military forces rounded up two thousand foreigners on the Chinese mainland and drove them like cattle into an internment camp. Langdon Gilkey, a young American university instructor, was among the businessmen, missionaries, educators, monks, and other Westerners crowded into the former mission compound. In order to survive, these foreign prisoners were forced to set up their own little civilization.

For two and a half years Gilkey watched the tiny society struggle to make life bearable. Initially enthused about his colleagues' ingenuity, Gilkey gradually came to see their underlying greed. He noted how internees tried to annex a few more inches of living space, how they cheated others out of rations allotted to the community, and how they refused to share the extra supplies that arrived from the outside world. People, he discovered, supported community decisions only as long as they profited personally. Beyond that they swindled and stole from their fellow prisoners to gain some personal benefit.

Gilkey came to the conclusion that people are not basically interested in the good of their society. They are fundamentally self-centered. When they have something to gain, they will cheat or attack others. This innate selfishness obviously hurt everyone, yet the little society was powerless to deal with it.[1]

What is wrong with man? Why do his dreams for a just and

prosperous society so often turn to nightmares of violence and greed?

Modern Views of Man

For nearly three centuries Western nations have accepted the Enlightenment dogma that man is basically good. His problems are external. What humanity needs is more public education and democratic institutions. Given these, man will create a better world for himself and his fellows. Every day in a host of ways the world is getting better and better.

In the nineteenth century Marxism arose to challenge this optimistic assessment of man's nature. Marx taught, and millions around the world now believe, that man's primary problem is economic exploitation. The rich take advantage of the poor. They treat the poor like animals in order to amass their own riches. But such cruelty always reaches a breaking point. The exploited will revolt and overthrow their oppressors. Revolution! That is the need of the masses.

Experience raises disturbing questions about the ideals of both democratic liberalism and revolutionary Marxism. Something more basic than ignorance or oppression is wrong with man.

People who refuse to take Christianity seriously often insist that Christians face the facts. But surely G. K. Chesterton was right when he said that human depravity is the one Christian doctrine that can really be proved. In our day of nuclear fears, family violence, international terrorism, and urban crime, who can in all honesty deny that something is dreadfully wrong with man?

The biblical term for the wrong in man is "sin." Novelists and playwrights have used the word so long for illicit sex that it has assumed a magnetic power in the world of entertainment. Movie magnates and advertising executives, aware of this force, have exploited the term for their own benefit.

Modern Americans are susceptible to this exploitation because they have been told that our Puritan fathers had an unhealthy attitude toward sex. And they want nothing to do with the repressive Puritans. Most people in the Western world today resent someone telling them what is right and wrong. Many of them believe that is what the Puritans did. So as soon as Christians mention "sin" they usually encounter rather stiff resistance to the continuation of the conversation. "Morality is what got the Puritans all messed up."

As a result of this resistance to the Christians' concept of sin and their use of the word, people are dying on every hand of a disease that they refuse to name. They have enlisted in a conspiracy of silence, apparently supposing that elimination of the word means elimination of the condition.

The subject of sin may be unpleasant, but like our doctor's report of our physical exam, it may be necessary if we are ever to regain our health. Before a physician can treat an illness effectively, he has to identify it. We all recognize the reluctance we feel to go for a physical examination, but we know that if we are ever going to feel better we have to—as we say—"take our medicine."

In that sense the Christian doctrine of sin is itself very good news. Our sickness can be treated. But many doctors in our society do not agree. They are telling people that our human condition is hopeless. They report that our problem is in our genes or our society or the stars; there isn't anything we can do about our condition. We are not responsible. But we are also not curable! That is not very good news.

In contrast to this determinism, the Christian doctrine of sin is good news indeed. Not only does the Christian faith confront man's basic sickness head on, it also affirms that man was meant for health, for a full and fruitful life. Christianity refuses to accept man's sorry condition as permanent. Under the right treatment his best days are ahead.

The Meaning of Sin

What does a Christian mean by sin? Without some understanding of this universal human condition, we are doomed to miss the whole point of the Bible's story and of the Christian faith.

Sin lies behind the call of Abraham, the exodus from Egypt, the Law at Sinai, the Davidic kingdom, the promise of Messiah, and the birth of Jesus Christ. The universality of sin makes the Christian gospel perpetually new.

As Christians use the term, sin means two things. First, sin is an act, or, at times, failure to act. It is either a failure to obey the law of God or some action contrary to the standards of God. This is the way we commonly use the word when we say someone "sinned" or "committed a sin." We usually think of such things as stealing or lying or adultery. And the Bible makes clear that these are sins. But behind the action there is the passion. This too is sin. Murder is the fruit of hatred; hate is the seed of murder. The two are inextricably united.

One of the most widely read works from the ancient world is Aurelius Augustine's *Confessions,* a kind of autobiography of his soul. At one point he tells about an incident from his childhood. Along with some friends he stole a load of pears from a tree near his home.

"I chose to steal," he said, "not because I was compelled to by poverty or hunger, but just from a bellyful of sin. . . . I didn't take pleasure in what I stole—I just enjoyed stealing and the sinning." He didn't even eat the pears. He threw them at the hogs, just because he knew it was wrong.

That was sin. It was an act, a wrong committed against his neighbor. But it was more. Slowly Augustine came to see that it was also an offense against God.

Christianity stresses that the conception of sin cannot be separated from the idea of God, because sin is not only contrary to the rules of God, it is an offense against God himself. Sin attacks not only the standards of God; it destroys the relationship with God. The Bible speaks of God as the source of all good. He is the very definition of truth and beauty and goodness. All that he has made is good, and the rules he gave were made to keep it good. So sin is more than an illegal act; it is also a personal affront.

That suggests that sin has another sense. First it is an act; second it is a condition. It is that state of rebellion against God in which we all live. Christians call this condition "original sin" because it is basic to human experience. It is the soil out of which the acts sprout and grow. It is the state of rebellion from which we launch all of our attacks against God's authority.

Christians also call it "original" because it is not just a personal problem. It afflicts all humanity. In his highly acclaimed *The Gulag Archipelago*, Aleksandr Solzhenitsyn says, "If only there were evil people somewhere insidiously committing evil deeds, and it were necessary only to separate them from the rest of us and destroy them. But the line dividing good and evil cuts through the heart of every human being. And who is willing to destroy a piece of his own heart?"[2]

Perhaps the most profound analysis of sin in all of literature is found in the first book of the Bible. The Genesis story of Adam and Eve tells how God placed the two of them in the Garden of Eden to work and care for it. He allowed them to eat of any tree in the garden with a single exception. They were forbidden to eat of the tree of the knowledge of good and evil.

In time, however, the crafty tempter came to Eve and asked, "Did God really say, 'You must not eat from any tree in the garden'?" His first move was to plant the seed of doubt by questioning God's word.

The woman followed his lead. She answered, "We may eat fruit from the trees in the garden, but God did say, 'You must not eat fruit from the tree that is in the middle of the garden, and you must not touch it, or you will die.' " Her added prohibition about touching the tree indicates that she had already begun to distrust God's goodness.

"You will not surely die," the serpent said to the woman. "For God knows that when you eat of it your eyes will be opened, and you will be like God, knowing good and evil" (Gen. 3:1–5). That was an effective move. He appealed to her pride. He suggested she reach beyond her assigned lot in life.

So she questioned her God-given life and followed her vanity. She seized the fruit and ate it. Then she gave some to Adam and he ate. The eyes of both of them were suddenly opened. They both knew that they were naked and unprepared to face

God. So they sewed fig leaves together in a futile attempt to cover their shame. But when they heard God walking in the garden, they hid from him.

Their act of sin led to their condition of sin. Rejection of God's law and their mad pursuit of something better resulted in their estrangement from God. So the Lord God banished them from the Garden of Eden.

This loss of paradise is the Bible's way of describing "original sin." It is the condition in which all people find themselves, separated from God yet longing for the inner contentment they once knew in his presence. We are like marionettes who have cut their own strings in the hope of finding another way to dance, and finding out too late that without the strings they cannot dance at all.

The Consequences of Sin

As a consequence of human sinfulness we all experience a sort of gravitational pull toward self-centeredness. It is much easier, as Langdon Gilkey discovered, to do the selfish deed, and to keep on doing it, than to do the generous and neighborly thing. Sinning is like skiing. The ease and excitement come on the way down the mountain. The trick is getting back up to the top. Most of us know that to get to the top we really need outside help.

Unfortunately, human help in overcoming this gravitational pull is limited. Most societies recognize the problem and try to restrict its damaging effects. They pass laws and create police forces and build prisons, but no society—as far as I am aware—has ever overcome the downward drag. The security of life and property must be one of the fundamental responsibilities of any government.

This human propensity also explains why sins are so habit forming. The first exciting experience of a sin makes the second easier. The second encourages the third, and so on until we find that we do not want to think of life without the fleeting pleasures of sinning. But we reach a point where we cannot give it up. We are hooked.

By that time it should be obvious that we cannot have the pleasure of sin without paying a price. Something dies in us when we insist on recapturing the delight of the forbidden fruit. We surrender a bit more freedom to the habit. We stoop a bit closer to the bestial level. Lower and lower we go until human freedom of choice is gone.

Sin, then, is a form of slow death. "A man reaps what he sows," said the apostle Paul. "The one who sows to please his sinful nature, from that nature will reap destruction" (Gal. 6:7–8). A child disobediently plays with matches and gets burned. A man abuses alcohol and gradually destroys his mind and his marriage. A woman cheats on her husband and loses her children, her home, and ultimately even her lover.

In recent years several prominent Americans have died from a strange disease called anorexia. It afflicts people in a mysterious way. They do not want food. They literally starve themselves to death, some of them in the belief that they will look better and feel better if they do not eat. Sin is a disease that works in a similar way. It convinces us that we will be happier and more admired by others if we will only refuse the food that might mean our health.

The ultimate consequence of sin is death. The two are inseparably linked. "The statistics on death," George Bernard Shaw, the British novelist, once said, "are quite impressive." The reason, says Christianity, lies in the nature of death. It is more than a biological fact. It is a consequence of sin.

If this poisonous fruit is ever to be uprooted we will have to consider drastic measures. Our lives are fields that primarily contain weeds. We cannot produce strawberries. We can mow the weeds, but that effort alone will never produce acceptable fruit. If we really want that fruit we will have to go deeper. We must plow up the whole field and start again with new plants.

The Christian view of sin is realistic because it explains both the dignity of man as a creature of God and the ruin of man in his self-chosen rebellion. Man has joined the ranks of the resistance. He is wandering through life far from his spiritual home, the only source of his true identity. Above every other concern, then, he needs to find his way back to his Father's house.

5

Speaking Terms

Robert Lewis Stevenson, a well-known poet and novelist, grew up in a home that confessed faith in God. As an adult, however, Stevenson lapsed into agnosticism. Only as he lay dying in faraway Samoa did he rediscover the faith of his childhood. Rheumatic and speechless—only forty-four years old—Stevenson held a notepad on his knees. On this he scratched simple messages for those attending him. Shortly before he died, he reached for the pad and scrawled: "Stately music; enter God."[1]

Christians have always insisted that faith is essential. People cannot possibly find fulfillment as long as they resist God. To find life and spiritual health they must look to the Hidden World. "Thou hast made us for thyself," Augustine, the influential bishop in fifth-century North Africa, once prayed, "and our hearts are restless until they find their rest in thee."

As birds are made for the air, human beings are made for life with God. You can thrust a bird under water and it will die. It is out of its element. It was not made for water; it was designed for air. Just so, when people try to survive without faith, they experience a slow death.

This faith is not a self-evident term. We need to ask, what is the Christian faith? What are the distinctive Christian beliefs and what difference do they make if we accept them?

The Meaning of Faith

It is necessary to press the meaning of faith because so many people in our secular society assume that faith is a kind of psychological key we use to open doors into an inner world of comfort and confidence. These people encourage the mystic moods of the soul, convinced that in them they can find true peace and freedom from stress. In all this their eyes are turned inward in the firm assurance that true religion is found in an attitude of the soul. They call it "faith."

Before we can seriously consider the Christian faith we have to confront this widespread line of thinking and make it clear that Christianity is not another path to "peace of mind" or "spiritual health." The men of faith we meet in the Bible are never introspective mystics, trying to work themselves into a mood of faith. On the contrary, they look away from themselves to the works of God in creation and history.

In Scripture, faith always rests on the good news of God's actions in our spare-time world. When Jesus urged men and women to "have faith in God," he never spoke of it as some mysterious power that normal people find incredible. Faith, in biblical terminology, is an attitude toward life open to all people. It is not something that strangely religious people pump up out of the deep recesses of their souls. It is a decision that all men make when they are confronted with some convincing testimony of God's action in time.

When the Bible speaks of faith it usually intends either of two related ideas. One is faith as beliefs. It stands for Christianity's description of reality. It appeals to a series of events that created certain fundamental convictions about God and man, and about Christ and salvation. These beliefs are basic to Christianity; they help to form and sustain that community of faith we call the church.

The other idea of faith, as the Bible uses the word, is trust. This idea goes beyond the rational element in Christian beliefs and emphasizes the relational element of faith. In this sense faith is akin to commitment, risk, and faithfulness, qualities of a special relationship between two people. It is what the Bible means by "knowing" someone.

These two meanings of faith are often intertwined in the Bible because the purpose of the truths *about* God is to lead men and women to personal trust *in* God.

It might help to think of the Christian faith as a letter. Sometimes families have a daughter who exchanges letters with a boyfriend living across the country. Occasionally, a young man will even propose marriage in one of these letters.

When the postman delivers the proposal, he is part of an event of immense importance. The event bears a message. When the daughter in the family reads the letter she understands the significance of the event and she faces a major decision. Will she marry the young man or refuse him?

If she says "yes" in her heart she will have to tell her family. When she does, the family is drawn into the relationship and immediately begins to discuss among themselves the meaning of the wedding and their part in the new family.

In a similar way, the basis of the Christian faith is first an *event* of immense importance. God sends his message to mankind and wraps it in an event: "God was in Christ, reconciling the world unto himself" (2 Cor. 5:19, KJV).

Second, the basis of faith appears as *gospel*. The witnesses of the event share what they have seen and heard. That is the Good News that we call the gospel. When men and women hear this story they either believe it or reject it. The telling of the story, like the proposal in the letter, calls for a personal response.

Faith is a "yes." It reflects a person's *trust* in the One who sent the message. And finally, faith appears as an explanation and application within the family. As the church reflects upon the meaning of the gospel, faith assumes the form of *beliefs* and creeds.

The event and the story are always fundamental to the Christian faith. Human feelings and moods are never primary. God comes first, and faith is always a response to God's initiative in Christ.

Some people find this particularity of the gospel offensive. Why can't all men everywhere have direct access to the truth? Christians see no value in arguing possibilities; they insist that wisdom deals with actualities. The offense of the gospel's historicity must remain.

This historicity also has a hidden value. It means the Word of God—event and gospel—is accessible to all who will listen to the story. Children may not grasp instructions. Stubborn men may not follow advice. Weak people may be unable to obey rules. But everyone can listen to a story. And those who listen may believe.

Because people are so prone to turn the gospel into something other than the Good News from God, we must stress its uniqueness. It is not some sort of Poor Richard's Almanac offering advice on raising children, making money, and serving God. It is not a short course on ethics, updating the Ten Commandments for moderns. It is not even a religious tract, prescribing five easy steps to God.

The gospel is first, last, and always good news about how God came to mankind and made his move for peace. It is an event that belongs on the front page of the Jerusalem newspapers in the Spring of A.D. 30. It is an event, a true story, a bit of history.

Faith As Trust

The gospel story, like the proposal in the letter, calls for a response. We will never understand the Christian faith if we try to examine it from a safe distance. It is not a frog's leg to dissect and classify. Truth, as Jesus used the term, is a personal reality. A man who wants to settle all the questions in his mind before he decides for or against the Christian faith is headed up a blind alley. He is adopting an attitude that makes it impossible for him to see realistically while looking at the Christian faith.

Some people refuse to take the gospel seriously because they try to judge Christianity by the standards of science. But that is foolhardy. Truth in a laboratory is determined by testing again and again under controlled conditions so that the experiment will yield the same results time after time. But Christianity—

like art and love and history—will not surrender to those standards. The Christian faith is not and never will be scientific in that sense of the word.

The gospel is the story of a unique event; there is no way to replay it. Neither is God an object like other objects. What would he look like under a microscope? The scientific method is not designed to render a judgment on Christianity.

Some people find that fact unacceptable. The successes of science have generated an unbecoming arrogance in some people. But that doesn't change the fact that science samples just a small slice of reality. What scientific instrument do we use to plumb the depths of Bach's musical genius or measure the mystery of a mother's love for her infant?

While Christianity cannot be tested by scientific methods, it is not, as a consequence, mere superstition. As one apostle put it, "we have not followed cunningly devised fables" (2 Peter 1:16, KJV). The gospel is good news. It is divine truth revealed in events that really happened. Christianity does not rest on myths. It welcomes inquiry. It is prepared to present evidence and state cases.

To score that point in a day of competing claims and widespread gullibility is important. Many people really do believe the old adage: "It doesn't matter what you believe as long as you're sincere." But anyone who will take time for second thoughts will realize that sincerely held convictions can be dead wrong.

Most Christians empathize with G. K. Chesterton when he says, "What we suffer from today is humility in the wrong place. Modesty has moved from the organ of ambition. Modesty has settled upon the organ of conviction; where it was never meant to be. A man was meant to be doubtful about himself, but undoubting about the truth; this has been exactly reversed." [2]

At the same time Christians ought not to overstate their case. They must hold fast to all that God has revealed, but they know that when they attempt to speak of God they are on the threshold of infinity and eternity.

In one of his last messages to the children of Israel, Moses said, "The secret things belong to the Lord our God, but the things revealed belong to us and to our children forever, that we may follow all the words of this law" (Deut. 29:29). One of the most difficult assignments in setting forth the Christian faith is sorting out the secret things from the revealed things.

The Christian faith rests upon adequate, not overwhelming, evidence. It is evidence to induce trust, not to settle lawsuits. An effective presentation of the gospel will always respect the freedom of the hearer simply because true faith must be personal faith. Everyone who enters the kingdom does so freely. That is the condition of any personal relationship. God is not interested in slaves within the kingdom; he wants children. That means genuine faith will always include choice, love, and commitment, realities of life that cannot be coerced.

The Language of Faith

In stating their beliefs, however, Christians face a major problem. They are confessing realities that are beyond normal human experiences. God is eternal, infinite, and invisible. How can human languages hope to convey meaning from realms beyond our five senses? And yet we have no other language. When we say God is a Father or a King or a Shepherd, we are using terms from human experience and these cannot possibly be accepted at face value.

The oldest, and perhaps the best, explanation of Christian language is the way of analogy. This rests upon the fact that God is the Creator of the universe and human beings are his creatures. There is a fundamental relationship between God and people. The Bible points to this relationship when it says God made man in his image, a kind of imperfect mirror of God's own character. This likeness between two people or two things we call "analogy."

The language of analogy expresses partial—not complete— similarity between two people or things. In speaking of God we use terms that carry only a limited correspondence of meaning. For example, when we say, "Mr. Simpson is certainly healthy," and a bit later, "Sun Valley is healthy," we mean Mr. Simpson is genuinely healthy. His blood pressure is normal. He has no infection. He is not overweight. We mean Sun Valley is conducive to health. It has fresh air and lots of sunshine. It is healthy in a derivative sense.

In a similar way, when we say, "God is powerful" and "Stalin is powerful" we mean God is omnipotent. He possesses power in its fullness. Stalin was only powerful in a derivative sense. Millions of people submitted to his authority. He did not have power in and of himself.

The language of the faith, then, is not the language of science or any other modern field of knowledge. It is the language of common people—more than adequate to lead us to the truth.

What makes the faith distinctively Christian? How can we sort out the genuine item from the thousands of substitutes and counterfeits in today's religious market? Are there, as a consequence of the revelation of God in Christ, special marks of the Christian faith? The bewildering variety of contemporary religious claims seems to argue against the possibility. Pluralism seems to be the order of the day. How can anyone speak of "the faith"?

That is not an easy question to answer. Through 2000 years Christians have expressed their faith in a host of forms and styles. Believers will probably always disagree on the best way to state their convictions. Is "total depravity," for example, an item of "the faith"? What about "eternal security"? Christianity is a historical movement, and determining the precise borders of any historical movement is a persistent problem. In many areas a believer should not pretend to speak for God.

When an antique hunter is in search of an heirloom he has in mind the hallmarks of the original. In our quest of the Christian faith, it might be helpful to list the hallmarks.

The Marks of Faith

The first hallmark of the Christian faith is Jesus Christ. What is God like? Look at Jesus Christ. What is human nature like? Check with Jesus Christ. What is God doing in the world? Consider Jesus Christ.

A total stranger to Christianity may find this focus on one

person a little surprising. After all, Mohammed taught submission to Allah. And Gautama Buddha pointed to Nirvana, the ultimate. Most founders of religions deliver to their followers some great truths. But in Christianity, Jesus is more than a teacher; he is the truth.

Christianity makes no sense apart from Jesus Christ. Faith in him sets Christianity off from the other major theistic faiths, Judaism and Islam. Christians have always considered him more than an influential rabbi or a prophet of God. Jesus made unique, exclusive claims about his relationship to God. "I am the bread of life," he said. Christianity arose when men and women found it impossible to deny his claims. They faced the startling possibilities of his assertions, and found that worship was the only appropriate response.

Worship of an apparent human being raises additional problems that we will have to face in time, but for now let this fact serve as a guide to the meaning of Christian faith: it concentrates on Jesus Christ.

The second hallmark of the Christian faith is the Bible. Almost all we know about Jesus Christ—his background in Judaism, his message to his contemporaries, his death at the hands of the Romans, the reports of his resurrection—comes from the Bible. The Old Testament creates the concepts of the Christian faith—creation, redemption, covenant, kingdom, Messiah—and the New Testament sets forth the center and climax of this faith: the Word, God's message, in flesh.

The Bible is something like a charter for the Christian faith. Like other movements, the church expanded into new times and new cultures. This growth meant adaptation to new languages and new patterns of thought. Under these conditions an institution can easily wander far from the purpose and intention of its founder. Christianity, however, continued to look to the Scriptures as the standard for faith. As a result, the church has discovered its errors time and again and returned to its original mission.

The third hallmark for identifying the Christian faith is the teaching of the church. The gospel creates a community of faith. Christians do not survive in lonely isolation; faith is followed by baptism into this community of believers. This fellowship of faith helps a believer grow and guards him from errors and excesses in his personal faith.

There is no other way. It might be tempting to try spinning out a new version of the faith from one's own private impressions of the Bible. This, in fact, is done. The term for that is not "Christianity" but "cult." The fact is anyone who claims to be presenting the Christian faith must constantly reckon with the witness of the church throughout the world and across the centuries.

In a rootless age, Christians must resist the temptation to reject tradition out of hand. The continuing existence of the Christian church and the creeds it has written over the centuries testify to the strength of that supranational community and the faith that sustains it.

Through the Christian centuries the churches wrote creeds and confessions to nurture the weak in faith and to guard the zealous from error. These statements of faith provide some balance for believers. They give contemporary Christians perspective, and help them sort out essential doctrines from faddish extremes.

The final hallmark of the Christian faith is what I like to call "good sense." Some people may prefer to call it "reason" in the sense of "reasonable." The label isn't as important as the thought. By "good sense" I mean the conviction every Christian has that the gospel "fits" reality as he has experienced it. The Word of God "fits" life as we have come to know it. It is appropriate.

This "good sense" is not the way mankind usually thinks. As we have seen, that is often at odds with God's truth. Our human thoughts are often not God's thoughts. The gospel often strikes a person as sheer foolishness. And yet there is another side of the matter.

Think of the story Jesus told about the son who demanded his inheritance from his father and left his home for a distant country. He spent all his money, and while feeding pigs he suddenly had second thoughts about life back home (Luke 15:11–17). The story simply says, "when he came to himself." Now what does that mean? In the experience of faith most Christians recognize a moment or a time of reflection when they come to see how the gospel makes sense to them. The Christian explanation of life and reality fits their own perceptions of reality.

Our perceptions do change. They are shaped by assumptions about reality that we absorb from our families, our acquaintances, and our culture. It seems, therefore, that the Christian faith must always be contemporary. It may challenge our assumptions or it may confirm our assumptions, but it cannot fail to engage them. Otherwise the gospel would never translate into faith. It would strike us as fantasy or nonsense, never the truth.

In his book, *Mere Christianity*, C. S. Lewis shows that men often surrender their convictions, or as we say "lose their faith," not because they are convinced by new evidence that their beliefs are fallacious, but because their emotions or imaginations overwhelm them.

Take, for example, a boy learning to swim. His reason tells him that an unsupported human body can remain afloat in water. He has seen dozens of people float and swim. But the whole question is whether he can go on believing this truth when the instructor leads him into the water and it is "sink or swim." Will he suddenly cease to believe it, listen to the voice of panic and go under?

The same thing happens with Christians. They confront the faith and accept it as a reasonable account of reality. But what happens? Within a few weeks they run into trouble or they meet people who ridicule their Christian commitment, and all of a sudden, says Lewis, their emotions "rise up and carry out a sort of blitz" on their beliefs. This rebellion of our moods is the test of our faith.[3] If we checked a hundred people who have lost their faith in Christianity, how many of them do you suppose turned away from the faith because some one reasoned them out of it? Don't most simply drift away?

Charles Williams once said, "The middle class in England did not wholly lose the habit of going to church until they acquired motor cars—so negligible in the end is intellect itself."

This assault on faith points up the need for what Lewis calls "training the habit of faith." A Christian must hold the great doctrines of Christianity before his mind daily. That is the purpose of the disciplines of daily prayer, Bible reading, and churchgoing. Faith needs a constant reminder. It will not remain alive in our minds unless we feed it regularly.

6

The Ultimate Ruler

Some years ago a manufacturer of children's clothing ran an advertisement in the *New York Times Magazine* inviting children to draw "what God looks like to you." Over 1700 drawings tried to picture God through the eyes of children. One of them by a five-year-old had two clouds. The caption read: "This is Mr. and Mrs. God. They look like clouds. They are very old."

Most of us, I suspect, tend to rely on rather foggy images of God. People on the streets of Western nations today think of God much as a seaman thinks of his lifeboat. He knows it is there, but he hopes he will never have to use it. That is not the faith that the Bible describes, because it is not the God whom the Bible discloses.

The first article of the Apostles' Creed, used in many Christian churches every Sunday, says, "I believe in God the Father Almighty, Maker of heaven and earth." But what is God like?

The Attributes of God

The words and phrases that Christians use to portray God are called "attributes." The term simply stands for the characteristics of a person. President Harry Truman, for example, was blunt. President Abraham Lincoln was courageous. Some attributes of people are positive and some are negative. Most of us appreciate the positive ones in people such as kindness and understanding, but we dislike brusqueness and greed.

When Christians speak of God as the Bible describes him they must hold in constant tension two fundamental convictions about him: First, God is unlike us. He is, as we say, "beyond" us. He is not man and man is not God. An unbridgeable gulf separates the Creator from his creatures. He is infinite and holy. We are finite and sinful. Theologians call this distinctiveness of God "transcendence," meaning he is "other" than we are.

Second, God is like us. He formed the universe and then created man and woman in his own image, capable of communion with him. As a consequence, human beings have the potential to know God and to share his purposes on earth. This created kinship is a reflection of what theologians call God's "immanence." Somehow he is present in this world that he has made.

Jeremiah, the ancient Hebrew prophet, linked these two basic truths about God in one of his messages to his people:

> "Am I only a God nearby," declares the Lord,
>   "and not a God far away?
> Can anyone hide in secret places
>   so that I cannot see him?" declares the Lord.
> "Do not I fill heaven and earth?"
>   declares the Lord.
>
> (Jer. 23:23–24)

When Christians describe this "far away" and this "nearby" deity they rely on these two basic convictions. Since God is unlike man, we have to speak in negative terms. We say that God is invisible when we mean he is not visible, or we say he is immutable, meaning not changeable, or infinite, meaning not finite, or incomprehensible, meaning not comprehensible. In this approach we try to describe God by removing from him the limitations of human existence. We call this the "negative way" to God.

At the same time, since God is also like man, Christians speak of God in positive terms. They say that God is almighty, perfectly good, omnipresent, and perfectly wise. In this approach to the attributes of God we take some human virtue and we raise it to eminence, that is, to the highest degree. So we call this the "way of eminence."

Thoughtful Christians have always confessed that every description of God is woefully inadequate. Attempting to describe God is like trying to picture a deepening Arizona sunset or a gliding gull over San Francisco Bay. Human language is simply incapable of depicting much of reality.

Still, Christians cannot remain silent. People who refuse to speak at all of the God beyond us go too far. He is veiled in mystery. That is true. But he has revealed himself. That is also true. He has spoken through the gardenia's fragrance and the galaxy's rhythm. But he has disclosed himself supremely through Jesus Christ. We cannot act as though nothing had happened. The fact that we cannot describe God fully does not consign us to silence. We have genuine, though not exhaustive, knowledge of God.

Let us speak, then, of this God who has revealed himself to us. In this chapter let us think of the God who is "far away" and in the next chapter of this same God who is "near."

God the Creator

In the Bible God comes first. Genesis 1:1 says, "In the beginning God . . . " These are the Bible's opening words. Nothing comes before him. But the God who is there—before all things—chooses to create. That is basic to the Christian view of God. The personal God of eternity freely chose to bring worlds into being. Nothing except God exists on its own. Not nature. Not man. Only God stands in self-sufficient splendor. The Christian faith, then, recognizes two fundamental categories of reality: God, the self-existent One, and the visible and invisible creation—the dependent universe.

If that distinction seems to make much ado about very little, appearances are deceiving. We may be forgetting that millions of people in the world today hold to pantheism, a faith that equates God with the universe. It teaches that the natural world is the self-unfolding of God. In this view God is depersonalized;

he is the name we give to Nature, the life force that surges through all that exists. He is not personal; he never talks; he hears no prayers. He is it.

In Christianity, however, the Creator stands in sovereign and self-sufficient majesty apart from the natural order. He made it, and he sustains it, but he is not it. The Westminster Confession of Faith, written in 1646, speaks for most Christians when it says God has "all life, glory, goodness and blessedness in himself." He alone is all sufficient. He has no need of any creature he has made.

In one of his books J. S. Whale tells a story about a youngster who was too restless to get to sleep one warm summer evening. He climbed out of his bed, crossed the room to the window, peeped through a chink in the blind, and saw his mother on the lawn playing croquet with some strange people. Naturally, she was entirely unoccupied with him, and it came to his little mind as a shock. He had always assumed that she existed for him and was, as it were, adjectival to him rather than a being who enjoyed an identity of her own. He realized now that she had a life of her own.[1]

In a similar way, God has a life of his own. Christian thought has always confessed this mystery of God's self-existence. It is basic to faith in the Creator.

The Christian also has to add a balancing truth. The Bible never considers creation merely a once-for-all event; it is also a continuous process. The God who brings galaxies and giraffes and goldfish into existence is also the Lord who sustains them. He is behind or within all physical processes, all reproductive powers, all harmonies and systems of nature.

In their indictment of Israel for unfaithfulness to the covenant with God, the Hebrew prophets time and again identify the Lord of the covenant with this omnipotent God of creation. "He who forms the mountains," Amos cries, "and creates the wind . . . He who made the Pleiades and Orion, and turns deep darkness into the morning . . . who calls for the waters of the sea, and pours them out upon the surface of the earth . . . the Lord is his name" (Amos 4:13; 5:8; 9:6, RSV). The basis of faith in the

Lord's steadfast purpose in Israel's history is his faithful presence in creation.

For the Christian, as for the prophets, "natural" never means "self-explanatory," but rather the stable, regular workings of the universe maintained by God. This explains the Christian rejection of deism, which professes faith in a Creator but finds no evidence of his maintenance of creation. Christian believers have never been happy with Alexander Pope's maxim:

> "The first Almighty Cause
> acts not by partial, but by general laws."

Christians deny that the vision of the First Cause and his "grand design" in nature is superior to the biblical portrait of the living God of Abraham, Isaac, and Jacob. Pope's Almighty Cause is unwilling or unable to administer the universe he has made. There is no hope for answers to prayers or miracles of deliverance. Man is alone in the universe. Are we to believe, then, that the deist's architect of Nature is superior to the Lord of Hosts?

Creation and Science

If we accept the Christian view of creation, are we not left without a rationale for science? Isn't the choice today either science or superstition? So many would have us believe. They recall the centuries-old warfare between science and Scripture. They do have a point. Science has forced Christians to change many of their ideas about God and the Bible. We now know, for example, that the earth is much older than our fathers once believed.

But it is also an established fact that modern science arose in Christian lands dominated by faith in a faithful God of creation. Many of the pioneers of modern science were devout Christians. There is no inherent reason why that cannot be true today. This is God's world and Christians should be among the first to understand and appreciate its mysteries.

Since the seventeenth century Christians have had to assume

the role of resistance fighters because so many modern men have had an unthinking confidence in science. They have made it the Ultimate Ruler and worshiped at its shrine.

Today we see the dangers of science much clearer than many did in an earlier age. We now know that it is not the whole of human existence. There are, in fact, threats to human survival on planet earth where science and technology attempt to operate without questions of purpose. Nuclear warfare and environmental pollution are only two of these dangers. Science, we now know, is far from the messiah we once envisioned. It is now clear that if science does not serve humane purposes rather than destructive ones, the human race is in imminent danger.

In contrast to this implicit faith in the wonders of modern science the Christian considers the universe a workshop of the will of God. According to Genesis, God saw that creation was good. It conformed to his intention. The Bible, then, does not describe the "how" of creation so much as the "why."

The Scriptures have a special way of stressing the dependence of creation upon the will of God: "By faith we understand that the universe was formed at God's command, so that what is seen was not made out of what was visible" (Heb. 11:3). Worlds came into being by the Word of God. The visible world is a product of powers from the Hidden World. God spoke and there was light. God lifted his voice and stars filled the heavens.

This Christian faith in the Maker of heaven and earth is unique, in the ancient world as well as in the modern one. It avoids both polytheism and naturalism.

We know that the ancient Sumerian civilization in Mesopotamia (about 3000 B.C.) held to a mythological polytheism. In the Sumerian creation stories the sea, the earth, and the deep appear as divinities—Nammu, Nin-mah, and Enki—engaged in a struggle to bring forth the created world. These myths, recited at great religious festivals, were repeated for purposes of magic. Their power was in the word itself.

The biblical story of creation, which may have borrowed some of the imagery of these myths, is sharply different in its message: Nothing exists apart from God. The Word of God appears, but the recitation and incantations are gone. Instead Genesis affirms that the Lord of the universe creates and sustains all things by the Word of God, by his self-revealing Power. Thus the regularity of the natural order—the presupposition of all natural science—is guaranteed by the God who speaks, and whose Word is power.

The Purpose of Creation

This description of creation cuts two ways. It not only challenges the polytheism of ancient Sumer, but it also refutes the naturalism of our own times. The modern idea of nature, with its accidental causes, is an impersonal universe. It knows only a dehumanized creation. Not so in Genesis. The biblical perspective is that behind all reality is the personal, transcendent God. The visible world is the effect of the Word of God. It is the expression of a purpose in the Hidden World. So according to the Bible, creation is purposeful. It offers us an answer to "why?" Let me illustrate.

We live in a mile-high city. During the winter months we see our share of snow. When the snows start to fall my wife puts an assortment of seeds in the bird feeder hanging under the apple tree near the house. The sparrows are there in no time. The starlings and red-winged blackbirds take a bit longer. The magpies, however, are reluctant to venture so close to the house.

I have often wondered, "Why should the big birds be so timid?" I finally got the courage to ask my wife, who is more a student of feathered creatures. She explained to me: "The sparrows are so much quicker than the magpies. They will come closer to the house for their food because they can zip away at the first sound of danger. The magpies are at a great disadvantage. It takes them forever to take off. They are like jumbo jets."

It seemed to make sense. Birds, I take it, do have what we call "instinct." In other words, behind their behavior is a purpose.

Naturalism gives us no answer to "why?" Its only alternative to a purposeful Creator is time and chance. It cannot explain to us why there should be anything at all.

Some years ago many people in the West held that evolution could explain everything. The universe, they said, developed by accident—all that nature needed was time. Given millions of years this world of apparent design pieced itself together.

You can often detect the absurdity of a position by translating it into cruder terms. Take a human parallel. One day the earth shook and trembled. Rocks flew in all directions. Some of them were piled high along the eastern seaboard of what is now the United States. Over the millennia winds blew and rains fell. Slowly the sun dried the mud until what we call the Jefferson Monument appeared just as it stands today. No human design was necessary, just forces of nature and time.

If you hold that mindless evolution accounts for the world we live in, that is how you think! Evolutionary science as an explanation of how the natural world operates is illuminating. But evolutionary thinking as an explanation of what the world is all about is nonsense. The absurdity of this line of thinking was highlighted by biologist Edwin Conklin when he said: "The probability of life originating from an accident is comparable to the probability of an unabridged dictionary resulting from an explosion in a printing shop."[2]

Christianity has always insisted that the supreme purpose of creation was man, the sole creature capable of communion with God. The Genesis story reaches its climax in God's breathing life into human flesh. Only Adam and Eve bear the image of God. Creation, then, must serve humane purposes. But man, the pinnacle of creation, must serve the purposes of God. Hymnist Robert Robinson asked:

> Mighty God, while angels bless Thee,
>   May a mortal lisp Thy Name?
> Lord of men, as well as angels,
>   Thou art ev'ry creature's theme.
> Lord of ev'ry land and nation,
>   Ancient of eternal days,
> Sounded thro' the wide creation
>   Be Thy just and endless praise.
> —*Mighty God While Angels Bless Thee*

The Christian doctrine of creation is more than a notion that God probably exists and has brought all things into existence.

As the Bible speaks of creation, it often aims at the will of man in order to drive men to the mercy of God. This is significant in our modern society filled with people who are ready to admit that God exists, but who have never felt the slightest impulse to bow in humble worship of him.

Martin Luther, who had a unique insight into the intention of Scripture, asked in his Small Catechism, what does it mean to believe in God the Father almighty, maker of heaven and earth? His answer: "I believe that God has created me and all that exists; that he provides me daily and abundantly with all the necessities of life, protects me from all danger, and preserves me from evil. For all of this I am bound to thank, praise, serve, and obey him."

This is most certainly true. When you turn from the clouds to the Bible you find that God is more than an old, old man. God the Creator is also more than the invisible Explanation of the ordered universe. He is the majestic Source of life itself and the awesome personal God before whom we must bow in grateful adoration. He does not ask for our reluctant acknowledgment of his power in nature. He has something far more radical in mind.

7

What Is God Like?

World War II was almost over. News of the armistice had reached the troops, but the actual order to cease fire was still on the way to the front. Then a bursting shell tore open a soldier's flesh. As his blood flowed out of the fatal wound, he said, "Isn't this just like God?" [1]

Everyone, it seems, has some concept of what God is like. Most human beings resist the thought of living in a world that is totally capricious. But what is the real Lord of all like? Are we left to our own personal impressions? Or is there some sure source that we can all trust for an answer?

The Personal God

As we have seen, the Christian Scriptures reveal two important truths about God. In one sense, he is unlike us. He is above us, transcendent in his creative power and majestic holiness. In another sense, he is like us. But how? What can the Almighty Creator possibly have in common with weak and egocentric human beings?

God, like man, is personal. By that we mean that he is on the side of persons rather than on the side of things. He is a "he"—a person—not an "it." He is aware of his existence. He thinks and decides and loves. As a person he can relate to us and we to him. That is important.

During the summer months children are constantly getting lost in the Rocky Mountains near our home. A party of sightseers may be enjoying the scenes of towering pines, cascading waterfalls, drifting white clouds, and blue skies. But when someone shouts, "Niki's gone!" the enjoyment of the crowd vanishes and concern for the lost child sends people in all directions calling, "Niki! Niki!"—fear written over their faces.

Why this sudden change of mood? Normal human beings recognize that one curly-haired child is more precious to parents and friends than a whole range of vast and towering mountains. A little girl can laugh and speak and pray and love but mountains can do none of those things.

I am not suggesting that this distinction between persons and things is always easy to recognize. It seems to come with maturity. When they were young, our children, like children everywhere, talked to their teddy bears. The soft little animals were a part of their world. But imperceptibly the years brought the children to that time in life when they no longer confused their stuffed toys with family members.

If we applied this insight to the life of faith, we would see how childish it is to treat God like a toy. A toy can only fulfill our imaginings. By the power of imagination it becomes what we want it to be. We project our dreams and impose them upon the unsuspecting teddy. But children, in time, learn that brothers and sisters have a mind of their own. Persons always do. And God does.

Some people find the thought of a personal God inferior to a concept of a God beyond personality. They refer to God as "the Absolute," "the Ground of Being," or "the Power of the Universe." It is the language of philosophy, however, not of religion. Abstractions like "the Absolute" are impersonal, more like powerful forces such as gravity and electricity. But how does one trust in force, or love a universal law? Ordinary people find no personal fulfillment in abstract concepts. Only a personal God can deepen friendship, love, and commitment within us.

Blaise Pascal, who lived during the era of the French Enlightenment, knew well the arguments for and against the existence of

God. He once wrote, "The God of the Christians is not a God who is simply the theory of geometric truths. This is the God of the pagans . . . . The God of the Christians is a God of love and consecration, a God who makes them feel their utter misery and his infinite mercy, . . . He makes the soul feel that its peace lies wholly in him, and that it has no joy save to love him." [2]

Once we accept the idea that God is personal, that he is like us in this important sense, then we must face the implications of that fact. It means we must surrender all of our attempts to project our dreams upon God. He is no teddy bear. We can't coax him, or cajole him, or control him by our prayers or our actions. We never earn the friendship of another human being, and we do not earn the favor of God.

This personal relationship with God works the other way, too. We must realize that he wants to fellowship with us, not control us or use us. He is not interested in overwhelming us. He will not compel our loyalty. He wants us to trust him and love him—freely.

If God is personal, then the deepest meaning of our lives lies not in abstractions and generalities, but in his personal purpose for them. What is it that he wants of us? There is no more significant question in all of life. If God has a purpose for us, that is the final meaning for living.

The Presence of God

This living, personal God is with us in two fundamental ways: He is with us as the Creator, the providential Ruler of the universe, sustaining our life from day to day. And he is with us as Savior, inviting us to consider our spiritual rebellion and to receive the offer of forgiveness extended to us in the gospel of Jesus Christ.

In the first case, God surrounds us with his presence; he envelops us in his creative life. He is our most basic environment. Just as the sea surrounds and sustains the tuna, or the air fills and supports the eagle in flight, so God is in the world he has made. He is over us, around us, and within us. In him we live and move and have our being.

William Blake expressed it this way:

> Think not thou canst sigh a sigh
> and thy Maker is not by;
> Think not thou canst weep a tear
> and thy Maker is not near.

For the Christian, then, the practice of the presence of God is not the projecting of some imaginary object from within his own mind and then seeking to realize that presence. It is rather the recognition of the real presence of the One who fills the whole universe.

The psalmist confessed that even his innermost thoughts were open to the One who is nearer than breath:

> Where can I go from your Spirit?
>   Where can I flee from your presence?
> If I go up to the heavens, you are there;
>   if I make my bed in the depths, you are there.
> If I rise on the wings of the dawn,
>   if I settle on the far side of the sea,
> even there your hand will guide me,
>   your right hand will hold me fast.
>
> (Ps. 139:7–10)

In one of his *Letters to Malcolm,* C. S. Lewis says: "We may ignore, but we can nowhere evade, the presence of God. The world is crowded with Him. He walks everywhere *incognito.*" [3] That he does.

This is dangerous ground, I know. The risks probably help explain the widespread neglect of the doctrine in some Christian circles. Many Christians fear mysticism, and not without reason.

What we must resist are two rivals to the biblical portrait of God: pantheism and deism. When we are among pantheists, who believe that an orchid or a honeybee is part of God, we must insist on God's distinctness. He is other than we, and all created things, are. But when we are among deists, who hold that the

Creator is an absentee landlord or an impersonal force, we must stress God's personal presence.

Perhaps the more pervasive reason we neglect the doctrine of God's presence is traceable to the restlessness it brings. He often comes to us not to comfort but to confront. The presence we evade is his presence in wrath. But isn't that the mark of reality? Deep down we know that nothing which always and everywhere agrees with us can have objective reality. Only sunsets in fantasyland never fade. Only dream girls never disagree with us. Real lovers always do. So with God. He is more real than our dreams.

In the second case, God's presence appears as Witness to his saving acts recorded in biblical history. According to Genesis, when Adam and Eve rebelled against God and tried to hide from him, he sought them out in an effort to mend the broken relationship. This pattern persists throughout the pages of the Bible: God, not man, makes the overture of love.

God came to Abraham in the land of Ur and he called him to a country far from his people. God appeared to the other patriarchs—at times in almost human form—in order to confirm his promise to Abraham and his children. He called the enslaved people of Israel out of Egypt and went before them as a fiery cloud, leading them by fire and smoke to the promised land. By creating a tradition of prophetic voices in Israel, God appeared in the spoken, then in the written Word. Throughout her history Israel recognized the presence of the Lord in fire, wind, and Word. From this story of God's persistent presence we can discover several of his dominant personal attributes.

The Love of God

First is the love of God. This appears many places in the Old Testament but most clearly in the experiences and the message of the prophets. The Lord often drafted a prophet for sacrificial service. He commanded him to demonstrate "the word of the Lord" by some painful experience.

Among the most difficult assignments was Hosea's. God told

him to lavish his love on a worthless woman. The prophet bound her to himself in the marriage covenant. Then, he felt the bitterness and pain of her desertion and adultery. The marriage was broken, yet God would not let Hosea forget. He sent him after her. Hosea pursued her and he wooed her until she returned to his home.

Through this experience, Hosea preached—and demonstrated—the love of God, love freely and lavishly given, yet squandered and spurned by his truant people. God's love was love that would not let his people go. He persisted until they returned to the privileges of the covenant they had broken.

While we can see the love of God reflected in Hosea's tragic love story, there is a significant difference in human love and God's love. We say that "love is blind"—but never totally. We love because we find something lovable in another. We expect some return for our devotion. But God's love is different. He loves without reasons—at least any reason known to man.

This thought appears many times in the Bible. In the book of Deuteronomy, Moses reminds Israel: "The Lord did not set his affection on you and choose you because you were more numerous than other peoples, for you were the fewest of all peoples. But it was because the Lord loved you . . ." (Deut. 7:7–8). "I loved you because I loved you." When we press for reasons we lose the love of God in the mystery of his hidden character. Unlike human love, God's love is undeserved, unconditioned, and totally free.

In his book *The Life of God in the Soul of Man,* Henry Scougal, the seventeenth-century Scottish minister, said, "God hath long contended with a stubborn world, and thrown down many a blessing upon them; and when all his other gifts could not prevail, he at last made a gift of himself." [4] That is God's love.

The Faithfulness of God

The test of such love is in another attribute of God. We call it God's faithfulness. The best reflection of it is again in marriage. In wedlock two people create a covenant. They commit themselves to one another "for better or for worse." In all kinds of situations, highs and lows, they promise to be faithful to each other. That is the picture the Bible uses to portray the faithfulness of God in his covenant, first with Israel and then with the church.

In modern times we define a host of relations by contracts. These are usually for goods or services and for hard cash. The contract, formal or informal, helps to specify failure in these relationships. That is one reason, however, why the terms of a contract cannot adequately express the relation between God and his people, and why the Lord did not establish a contract with Israel or with the church. He created a covenant. There is a difference.

Contracts are broken when one of the parties fails to keep his promise. If, let us say, a patient fails to keep an appointment with a doctor, the doctor is not obligated to call the house and inquire, "Where were you? Why didn't you show up for your appointment?" He simply goes on to his next patient and has his appointment secretary take note of the patient's name who failed to keep the appointment. The patient will find it harder the next time to see the doctor. He broke an informal contract.

According to the Bible, however, the Lord asks: "Can a mother forget the baby at her breast and have no compassion on the child she has borne? Though she may forget, I will not forget you!" (Isa. 49:15).

The Bible indicates that the covenant is more like a marriage bond or the ties of a parent to his child than it is a doctor's appointment or a purchase agreement. One member's failure does not destroy the relationship. It rests upon the character of the parties. It puts no conditions on faithfulness. It is the unconditional commitment to love and serve.

God's covenant is the heart of his relationship to men. Like a human marriage God's covenant calls for faithfulness. As Israel's history shows, however, the chosen people proved faithless. They turned from the Lord, time and again, and trusted in powerful nations and foreign gods. Israel committed spiritual adultery. Yet, even in the face of Israel's infidelity, God proved faithful.

In his book *The Distinctive Ideas of the Old Testament,* Norman

Snaith says, "Wonderful as is His love for His covenant people, His steady persistence in it is more wonderful still. The most important of all the distinctive ideas of the Old Testament is God's steady and extraordinary persistence in continuing to love wayward Israel in spite of Israel's insistent waywardness." [5]

Again the contrast with human faithfulness is striking. Human beings are never free from the temptation to unfaithfulness, the infidelity of the heart. Yet when someone proves untrue to us, we are quick to judge. We are ready to punish. But when Israel went too far, and God had to bring judgment upon his people, God was still true to his promise. A remnant of Israel and Judah survived the exile. God would not be untrue to himself. He would fulfill his loving purpose for Israel even when Israel was the major roadblock to it.

The Righteousness of God

The consequence of this faithful love of God for humanity introduces a third revealing characteristic of God. We call it *justice* or *righteousness*. Both terms are widely misunderstood. In our day *justice* has come to mean "my rights." And *righteousness* often stands for a stuffy legalism paraded by religious people.

In the Bible, however, righteousness reveals an unusual side of the character of God. The root of the term suggests whatever "is as it should be." But what can that mean when we say God is righteous? That he plays the game according to the rules? That he is a perfect gentleman? Not exactly. God made the rules. He not only defines what is moral; he is the source of morality. He is not only righteous; he is concerned that his people also be righteous. Righteousness is not only a part of his personal character; it is an essential part of his government of the world.

In the Bible, poets, prophets, and scribes unite in asserting God's relentless opposition to injustice and the oppression of men. God's wrath is against the man who exploits his neighbor. One episode in the life of David, Israel's most illustrious king, graphically illustrates this attribute.

David had sinned grievously against God by taking Bathsheba

to his bed and then attempting to cover his affair by arranging the death of her husband, Uriah. The sin, however, was not hidden from the prophet of God. Nathan told the king a story about a rich man who seized a poor neighbor's only lamb. And David's anger was kindled. He knew that the poor man was not beyond the attention of the righteous God. He, in fact, is a special object of God's care. Nathan had only to draw the parallel to Uriah to incite David's repentance.

This care of God for the oppressed is only a short step from his deliverance of the oppressed. The righteous God who cares for suppressed people acts to deliver them.

> Who is like you, O Lord?
> You rescue the poor from those too strong for them,
> the poor and needy from those who rob them.
> (Ps. 35:10)

In a world that is not as it should be the righteous God is at work setting things right. That is simply a reflection of his character.

The Christian, then, believes that God is more than a personal impression at death. With the Bible he holds that God is loving and faithful and righteous—like any admirable person, only more so. Much more.

8

The Dark Side of Life

In the early 1950s Charles Templeton was one of the big names in North American evangelism. He started preaching in his twenties at Youth for Christ rallies. From 1951 to 1954 he served as the chief evangelist for the National Council of Churches, preaching to audiences of up to 70,000 in places such as Soldier's Field in Chicago, the Rose Bowl in Pasadena, and Radio City Music Hall in New York City.

In 1957, however, Templeton quit the ministry. He no longer had a message to preach. He entered television and then newspaper journalism before accepting a position as news director for the Canadian Broadcasting Corporation. Quite simply, Charles Templeton lost his faith.

"I looked at the world," he said in 1978, "and it doesn't seem to me that it bespoke a God that could be described as father. It seems to be a universe indifferent to man and to all creatures." To support this estimate he cited natural disasters such as a typhoon that smashes an area, killing thousands, old and young, and leaving others unsheltered, diseased, and starving. "When I see that kind of prodigal waste," he said, "it doesn't look to me like the act of a father." [1]

Sometimes faith is all uphill. Through the centuries Christians have confessed faith in "God the Father Almighty, Maker of heaven and earth." But is that realistic? So many things happen that, if we attribute them all to God, we would seem to make of him a repulsive monster, not a loving father.

The Barriers to Belief

Is it true that all things have meaning and purpose in God's sight? In the bitter experiences of life can I believe that God is using these things somehow to work out his purpose? That is the way most people encounter what we usually call "the problem of evil." It is the great roadblock to faith.

Alfred, Lord Tennyson, who often longed for the assurance of life's meaning, wrote:

> O, yet we trust that somehow good
> Will be the final goal of ill,
> To pangs of nature, sins of will,

> That nothing walks with aimless feet;
> That not one life shall be destroyed,
> Or cast as rubbish to the void,
> When God has made the pile complete.

> So runs my dream; but what am I?
> An infant crying in the night;
> An infant crying for the light;
> And with no language but a cry.
> —*In Memoriam A. H. H.*

The Loss of the Mysterious

This barrier to belief is not new. The Old Testament prophets and psalmists show clearly that men and women struggled with it in ancient Israel. What makes the argument so powerful today is the social context in which men raise it.

The Western world today, as we have seen, is pervaded by secularism, a style of life and a pattern of thought based upon the assumption that the meaning of life can be discussed and decisions can be made without any reference to God. In a secular world people are conditioned to resist all thoughts of God. We can find several reasons for this.

In the first place, modern men and women seldom think of God because they are preoccupied with secular concerns. Many people are just too busy to worry about the existence of God. This preoccupation is usually a product of affluence. We are swamped by things—things to see; things to buy; things to finance; things to repair; things to store; things to dump.

Jesus once put his finger on our fevered infection. In his parable about the sower he described some people in whom the "worries of this life" choke out the Word of God. Our constant focus on the here-and-now dulls our sense of spiritual reality.

In the second place, modern people find faith in God difficult because they are conditioned to think of the world as though there were no God. Few people today assume that God controls the weather. We all know that atmospheric conditions are caused by high and low pressure systems, humidity levels, and wind currents. Who among us trace our illnesses to God's activity? We know all about viruses, carcinogens, and cholesterol in our bodies. We no longer need to assume God's existence for health or healing. We have pills for that.

In the third place, contemporary culture is biased against faith in God because we suffer from atrophy of a sense of wonder. Pioneering scientists seldom lose this sense of awe before the universe but common people often do. We tend to believe that all the mystery goes out of a flower when botanists name its parts. We no longer catch our breath in the light of a dazzling sunset. Television reproduces the scene nightly at five and ten.

These cultural attitudes are so deadening because, as sociologist Peter Berger once pointed out, most of what we "know" we take on the authority of others. Only as others continue to confirm this "knowledge" for us, will we accept it as plausible. In Western societies this puts God at a decided disadvantage because he has been all but banned from public life.[2]

For all these reasons, then, the tragic side of life strikes us as a powerful put-down of faith in God.

Human Responsibility

When suffering comes it is usually either of two types. Most of our pain comes from human action or inaction. This includes crimes, automobile accidents, wars, broken marriages, some starvation, and much of our ill health. All the great genocides of this century—the holocaust under Hitler, the purges in the Soviet Union under Stalin, and the extermination of Ugandans by Idi Amin—are traceable to human decisions. As a race, human beings show an amazing capacity to inflict suffering upon each other.

Awareness of this violence in human nature by no means solves the problem of pain, but it does demonstrate how often we are perpetrators of pain as well as the victims of it.

A lesser proportion of our suffering comes from so-called natural disasters—earthquakes, cyclones, tidal waves, and droughts. In these instances no human being seems directly responsible for the mindless deaths of infants and the lifelong suffering endured by innocent victims.

In those cases where some human being shares in the responsibility for suffering it may be easier to direct our rage toward another person. But how can God be exempt from blame in the tragedies of nature? If a good and omnipotent God created the world, why is it so full of pain? Perhaps John Stuart Mill, the philosopher, posed the problem in its sharpest terms: "If God is able to prevent evil and does not, he is not good. If he would prevent evil and cannot, he is not almighty."

Many, like Charles Templeton, have felt this dilemma so deeply that they have renounced their faith and have chosen instead some form of courageous unbelief. But what sort of unbelief is this that continues to point a finger at God, even while denying his existence? Doesn't genuine unbelief stop complaining and simply accept a meaningless universe?

C. S. Lewis found this so. While attempting to deny the existence of God during his student days, he discovered a major flaw in his argument. "My argument against God," he explained, "was that the universe seemed so cruel and unjust. But how had I got this idea of *just* and *unjust?* A man does not call a line crooked unless he has some idea of a straight line. . . . Thus, in the very act of trying to prove that God did not exist— in other words, that the whole of reality was senseless—I found I was forced to assume that one part of reality—namely my idea of justice—was full of sense." [3]

Angry atheism, it turns out, is too simple. If the universe is without meaning, then we would never find it out. True atheists do not argue with God about right and wrong. They do not believe such things exist. So unbelief is not a productive approach to the problem of pain.

God's Presence in Pain

The Christian faith—as far as I have been able to determine— has only a partial answer to the problem of evil. A great deal of mystery remains. Most Christians, however, lean upon several fundamental truths.

First, Christianity acknowledges the reality of evil. When Jesus taught his disciples to pray he included the petition: "Deliver us from evil." The Christian faith, unlike some other religions, never regards evil as an illusion. It is not a misguided way of thinking, a problem of human perception of reality. It is there, an actual fact of human existence.

At the same time, Christianity has never endorsed a doctrine of dualism—a view of reality that holds two conflicting eternal principles: one good, the other evil. This dogma appears in some ancient religions such as Manicheanism and Gnosticism. But whatever Christians have done with the image of Satan, they have expressed few doubts that he is limited in his evil activities by the power of Almighty God.

In brief, then, Christians insist that evil is real. It is not some sort of racial nightmare that will eventually vanish. But neither is it ultimate. God is. For his own mysterious reasons God allows evil to operate.

Second, Christianity teaches that man is endowed by God with a fundamental freedom. By that term we do not mean that men and women can do what they wish. They are limited by their finite existence. By "freedom" Christians mean that people are responsible before God for their lives. They are free from excessive external constraints to good or evil. They are not helpless victims of heredity or environment. They are responsible for their choices.

This reminder of my responsibility for my life tends to shift the problem of evil a bit. It takes it out of the realm of theories and makes it a personal matter. That is what Jesus did. Some of his contemporaries pointed to a recent tragedy. A group of Galileans were in the temple offering sacrifice when Herod's soldiers suddenly fell upon them and slaughtered them on the spot. How could God let that happen? Jesus said, "Do you think that these Galileans were worse sinners than all the other Galileans . . . ? No! But unless you repent, you too will all perish" (Luke 13:1–5).

Notice how Jesus shifted the question from, "God, how could you let this happen?" to "God, why doesn't it happen to me?" He brought his curious listeners to their own responsibility before God. He would not let them use the problem of evil as a cover for their own sin. We all tend to forget that we are a part of the problem of evil.

Third, the Scriptures speak of a God who is moved by human suffering. He is not a heartless observer. He cares and comes to sufferers' aid. At the end of his prophecy, Habakkuk, who had wrestled so vigorously with the problem of pain, wrote,

> Though the fig tree does not bud,
>   and there are no grapes on the vines,
> though the olive crop fails
>   and the fields produce no food,
> though there are no sheep in the pen
>   and no cattle in the stalls,
> yet I will rejoice in the Lord,
>   I will be joyful in God my savior.
>   (Hab. 3:17–18)

Much later, Jesus, knowing of his own approaching agony, told his disciples, "In this world you will have trouble. But take heart! I have overcome the world" (John 16:33).

Christians have always found this victory in Jesus' cross. There, faith says, God entered into the travail of sin and suffering and moved decisively for man and his salvation. Because of this crucial act, men and women can find assurance of God's presence and power in dark valleys of pain.

What God gives his people is not answers; he gives them his presence. That is what the Book of Job illustrates so effectively. Job wanted an answer to the problem of the suffering of the righteous. The book shows that the struggle was unfolding on two levels—an earthly level and a heavenly level. Job had no access to the heavens. And God never tells him about the heavenly level. Instead he comes to Job. So the climax of the book sounds in Job's words: "My ears had heard of you but now my eyes have seen you" (Job 42:5).

Finally, Christianity promises a life to come where justice will prevail. Without this hope the problem of evil may well be insoluble. But the Christian hope is not something added to faith; it is part of faith's substance. The mysteries of tragedy, evil, pain, and injustice are not resolved in this life. At present we do not see everything subject to God. But we see Jesus. He is the promise of the life to come.

Faith and the Future

In the end, then, it is not the mere presence of pain that makes faith in God difficult. Otherwise, people would find it difficult to believe in God because of the discomfort they feel in carrying their own groceries from the store. What does bother us is the occurrence of evil on a scale so great that we cannot imagine anything that would compensate for it.

The patient in the dentist's waiting room has little difficulty imagining the time when his suffering will prove worthwhile. But one's three-year-old grandson dying of cancer is another matter. We find it more difficult to imagine any situation that could justify that pain. Even God, we feel, cannot make that not matter. That is the real problem of evil. It is pain on a scale too great to conceive any way that even God can justify it.

But let us suppose—just suppose—that God's resources are so much beyond what we can imagine that he can produce a situation in which we can honestly say, "I see now that even the butchery of six million Jews doesn't matter. This is why he didn't do what I would have done if I had had the power to strike dead every Nazi in order to prevent it." [4]

This line of thought does not solve the problem of evil. But it points in the direction of a solution. The idea goes back to Jesus. "A woman," he once said, "giving birth to a child has pain because her time has come; but when her baby is born she forgets the anguish because of her joy that a child is born into the world" (John 16:21).

William Cowper, the hymn writer who encountered the problem of evil personally and profoundly, wrote:

> God moves in a mysterious way
>   His wonders to perform;
> He plants His footsteps in the sea,
>   And rides upon the storm.

> Judge not the Lord by feeble sense,
>   But trust Him for His grace;
> Behind a frowning providence
>   He hides a smiling face.

The problem of evil, then, is the problem of faith. Do we believe in a God big enough to make any suffering seem worthwhile? The overwhelming testimony of the Bible is that when countless men and women living in ancient times encountered the painful side of life, just as we do, they anchored their lives to just such a faith.

9

The Invasion

The world's major religions trace their origins to a few great leaders. The figures of Buddha, Moses, Mohammed, and Christ tower over the faiths of the world's people. The vast majority of people on earth have been influenced by these religious leaders.

Even the simplest introduction to these faiths, however, reveals that the place of the leader in a religion varies greatly. The Buddha (Gautama) is the most elusive of the founders. His influence among Buddhists is limited to his teaching. His life and personal history are almost incidental. Moses stands out sharply as a major figure in Jewish religion but Jews would never think of pointing to Moses as the founder of their religion. Mohammed is the supreme prophet of the Muslim world and his teachings are the authoritative voice for Islam, but no Muslim would refer to Mohammed as "Lord" or "Savior."

Obviously, Jesus Christ's relation to Christianity is unique. He is central. Only in Christianity is the personality of the founder absolutely essential to the faith. Remove Jesus Christ from Christianity, prove that the gospel story is a myth, and the Christian faith crumbles into worthless dust. You might retain an ethical system of some sort, but no controlling influence like that in Christianity during the last two thousand years would remain.

Why? What makes Jesus Christ central to Christianity? Who do Christians say he is? The answer to that question pierces to the heart of the Christian message. The church in every century, and in every place, has not only followed his teachings. It has worshiped him as a living Lord.

If we stop and think about that fact for a minute we may feel the shock of it, just as Jesus' earliest followers did. C. S. Lewis put it best when he wrote: "Among the Jews there suddenly turns up a man who goes about talking as if He was God . . . . Now let us get this clear. Among Pantheists, like the Indians, anyone might say that he was a part of God, or one with God: there would be nothing very odd about it. But this man, since He was a Jew, could not mean that kind of God. God, in their language, meant the Being outside the world Who had made it and was infinitely different from anything else. And when you have grasped that, you will see that what this man said was, quite simply, the most shocking thing that has ever been uttered by human lips." [1]

The Life of Christ

Outwardly, Jesus' life was like thousands of others in the land of Palestine during the era of Roman occupation. He was born in the village of Bethlehem and raised in a Galilean town called Nazareth. Like most eldest sons in those days, he was probably apprenticed in the family trade—in his case carpentry.

A time came, however, when he left home to travel about Galilee, Samaria, and Judea—the three districts of Palestine— preaching, healing, and teaching. He joined the ranks of itinerating rabbis in Israel. His career, however, proved brief and tragic. He ended up on a Roman cross outside of Jerusalem at Passover time.

The simplicity of the story only accents the urgency of the question: Why did people come to worship Jesus of Nazareth? Some historians have tried to present Jesus as just another Jewish rabbi. That is surely the place to start. He was Jewish and people did consider him "a teacher sent from God." But we cannot make Jesus intelligible until we also see him as the instigator of the Christian movement.

The Claims of Christ

Strangely, the Jesus movement began with some things Jesus said and did that most Jews considered blasphemy. The word is not too strong. It suggests defamation or injury to the reputation of God. That fits, because many of the things Jesus said and did were shocking to religious people. He spoke of God in the most intimate terms and claimed to have unique divine authority.

Take, for example, his habit of referring to God as *Abba*. In his native language, Aramaic, that meant *Daddy*. He used the expression in his own prayers and he taught his followers to use it in theirs (Mark 14:36 and Matt. 6:9).

Most pious Jews, however, found that kind of chumminess shocking. They knew the commandment against taking God's name in vain and they had come to hold God's name so sacred that they never spoke it aloud. They chose to refer to God in polite euphemisms such as "He Whose Name Makes the Hair on the Back of the Neck Stand on End." Rabbinic law held that anyone heard uttering the name of God aloud was to be stoned to death for blasphemy. Yet that is the culture in which Jesus used a family nickname—Abba—to refer to God.

Jesus reflected a similar shocking attitude toward Jewish customs. Take sabbath observance as an example. The Jews considered it a holy day. One sabbath, however, Jesus and his disciples were hiking through a field of grain. When they grew hungry they dared to pick some of the grain to eat. The religious authorities caught them in the act and demanded an explanation.

Jesus answered that King David had sanctioned a similar action by his companions. After all, said Jesus, the sabbath was made for people, not people for the sabbath. "The Son of Man is Lord of the sabbath" (Luke 6:1–5). Was he claiming authority over the sabbath? Isn't that a clear case of blasphemy?

Take one more provocative act, Jesus' practice of forgiving people's sins. According to the Old Testament, only God can forgive sins against God's law. And yet once when Jesus returned to his hometown, some men brought to him a paralytic man lying on a mat. When Jesus saw the man he said to him: "Take heart, son; your sins are forgiven" (Matt. 9:1–2). You can imagine what the teachers of the law thought: "This is blasphemy."

Jesus' conflict with traditional religion in Israel came into sharpest focus in Pharisaism. The Pharisees were diligent students of the Scriptures. They were convinced believers in God. They were determined that their traditions should be obeyed in the tiniest detail.

But somehow, in spite of their passionate devotion to the Law, they had lost touch with the living God. Religion had become for them a performance of rituals and duties aimed at gaining God's favor. Anyone unwilling to conform to their concept of religion fell under their scorn. They had come to think of God as a heartless taskmaster rather than a caring Father. Pharisaism illustrates how easy it is for any religion to become an obstacle rather than a highway to God.

Jesus never revolted against this Judaism offhandedly. He tried to remain a loyal son of Israel, but he could not allow the damaging effects of Pharisaism to go unchallenged. It stood in the way of men and women seeing God as a gracious and forgiving Father.

Jesus, however, was more than a religious reformer. He dared to confront the Pharisees because he claimed an authority higher than their traditions. Jesus was convinced that he was the Savior of the world. In him men and women found a new and living way to God. "I am the light of the world," he said (John 8:12). "I am the way and the truth and the life" (14:6). Constantly he claimed to stand at the center of life. "Come to me," he said, "all you who are weary and burdened, and I will give you rest" (Matt. 11:28).

When we compare these words with the promises of the prophets in Israel, we see that Jesus was assuming a position that only God can take. Our estimation of Jesus cannot ignore this claim. If Jesus is mistaken in this central conviction, then we must consider him an egotistical religious teacher—sincere perhaps, but fundamentally misguided. Misguided to the point of insanity.

But when we survey Jesus' life and teachings we find no trace of such egotism. He sets himself at the center of life, not for selfish or deranged purposes, but because he humbly recognizes that in the eternal order of reality he belongs there.

Christ's Impact

This claim to divine authority was more than a personal, psychological quirk. Hundreds of people who crossed Jesus' path recognized it as true. They found themselves confronted by a major decision. Would they join the scoffers who dismissed him as a troublesome dreamer, or would they follow him to God and be transformed?

One man, for example—a wealthy tax collector named Zacchaeus—invited Jesus to his home and before the Master left Zacchaeus found he had to reorder his whole lifestyle, beginning with the way he valued his money. When he expressed his willingness to change, Jesus said to him: "Today salvation has come to this house" (Luke 19:1-9).

Such encounters were almost common. Peter, one of the disciples who had seen scores of men and women turned around by their encounters with Jesus, tried to express what he had come to think of Jesus. It was almost the unthinkable thought. But once under Jesus' questioning he blurted out, "You are the Messiah, the Son of the Living God" (Matt. 16:13-16). Jesus didn't deny it.

In recent years men have tried to present Christianity as something charming and popular. They have painted Jesus as a religious teacher with unusual insight into human nature, but one without offense. That is absurd, for Christ went about Galilee giving offense to all kinds of people. This young Jew was so inflammatory in his message that he was thrown out of synagogues, hounded from place to place, and finally arrested as a public nuisance.

"Let us," Dorothy Sayers once said, "in Heaven's name, drag out the Divine Drama from under the dreadful accumulation of slipshod thinking and trashy sentiment heaped upon it, and set it on an open stage to startle the world into some sort of vigorous reaction." [2] The Christian centuries echo with a resounding, "Amen!"

Jesus' ministry among men reached a climax in his death and secured for him his unique place in Christianity. Death came as no surprise. He apparently expected the opposition of the Jewish authorities to lead to his destiny. More than once he mentioned his approaching death to his disciples. He seemed to anticipate his shameful treatment in Jerusalem. He knew his claim to divine authority was not a popular one. At his trial the Jewish leaders told the Roman governor, "We have a law, and according to that law he must die, because he claimed to be the Son of God" (John 19:7).

When the crucifixion came, it struck his disciples as a tragic enigma. Death somehow seemed a contradiction to the life of Jesus. He had been so often the victor. Why was he now so obviously death's victim?

The disciples discovered the answer to that question in the surprising sequel to the crucifixion, Jesus' resurrection from the grave. After three days in the tomb, he returned to them. On several occasions he offered them proof that death could not hold him. They saw then the significance of the cross. This extraordinary thing was nothing less than an act of God. Jesus died an atoning sacrifice for the sins of men and was raised again to life by the power of God in order to provide forgiveness and spiritual power for all who believe in him.

On the day of Pentecost, when the Holy Spirit descended upon the disciples and empowered them to witness boldly of the significance of Jesus' life, death, and resurrection, Peter dared to tell his Jewish kinsmen, "God has made this Jesus, whom you crucified, both Lord and Christ" (Acts 2:36).

That was the birth of the Christian gospel. As Michael Green, the Anglican scholar, once put it, the disciples believed that within the confines of a human life "the Ultimate had become embodied, the Absolute had become contemporary." [3] The Lord of the Hidden World had visited ours.

Faith in Jesus as a supernatural Savior courses through the twenty-seven books of the New Testament and makes them one in witness and intent. One passage from the apostle Paul, perhaps based on an early Christian hymn, will speak for hundreds of other texts:

> Christ Jesus . . .
> Who, being in very nature God,
>   did not consider equality with God
>   something to be grasped,
> but made himself nothing,
>   taking the very nature of a servant,
>   being made in human likeness.
> And being found in appearance as a man,
>   he humbled himself
>   and became obedient to death—
>   even death on a cross!
> Therefore God exalted him to the
>   highest place
>   and gave him the name that is
>   above every name,
> that at the name of Jesus every knee
>   should bow,
>   in heaven and on earth and under
>   the earth,
> and every tongue confess that Jesus
>   Christ is Lord,
> to the glory of God the Father.
>   (Phil. 2:5–11)

The Birth of Christology

After the passing of the apostles, during the early centuries of church history, Christian believers faced a disturbing problem: How do we describe this profound reality we call "God in flesh"? Believers quickly discovered that it is all too easy to fall into some misleading answers to that question.

On one hand, if they answered that Jesus was some divine being, then their simple logic forced them to add that Jesus only seemed to be a human being. Examples of the gods disguised in human form, coming to earth to accomplish this or that divine mission, and then returning to the divine realm, were too common in the ancient world to be ignored.

Was Jesus born of a virgin? So were half the members of the Pantheon. Did Jesus ascend to heaven? So did Hercules. Jesus, it seemed, fit the pattern of the Greek gods. So some misguided believers said that Jesus only seemed to be a man; he was really a god of some sort.

But thoughtful Christians rejected such views and labeled them *docetic*—from the Greek word *dokein,* meaning to seem or to appear. They recognized the problem with this line of thinking. It undercuts the gospel.

If Jesus only appeared to be human and never really lived among men, if he was a ghost, then the gospel is reduced to a myth. After all that is what the stories of the Greek gods were. Only a child took them as facts. But the gospel means "good news." Christians were claiming that in the life of Jesus—a historical person known by thousands of people—God actually entered history and provided salvation for men.

On the other hand, some early would-be Christians answered the question about Jesus by insisting that he was really and fully man. God simply empowered him by a special gift of his Spirit. This view is called adoptionism because it holds that God adopted Jesus for his purposes.

That, too, was plausible. Certain passages in the New Testament supported it. We can think of instances when Jesus was angry, hungry, or tired. The Gospels speak of his growing up through childhood and adolescence, of his eating and drinking, or his death and burial. So in the early church there were those professing Christianity who insisted that the answer to the "Who is Jesus?" question was a man, only a man.

The trouble with this view is that it, too, empties the gospel of its power. If the person who died on the cross was only a human being, then his death could only be a tragic accident. He might be a model of selfless dedication, a devotee of noble ideals who inspires others to similar nobility, a kind of Jewish Socrates. But he would still be nothing more than an example.

If that were so, then where is the good news for sinners? Where is the atonement for sin? Where is the overthrow of evil? The church rejected this view of Jesus, just as it had the opposite teaching of the docetists. It examined the portrait in terms of the gospel and found it a distortion.

The classical Christian teaching about Christ—called Christology—developed through a lengthy process culminating in the middle of the fifth century. A series of church councils worked through a maze created by a number of well-meaning Christian thinkers. This Christology does not make logical or mathematical sense. It wasn't supposed to.

The climactic council at Chalcedon in Asia Minor (today's Turkey) asserted that Jesus was completely and fully human. It also affirmed that Jesus was completely and fully God. Finally, the council confessed that this total man and this total God was one completely normal person. In other words, Jesus combined two natures, human and divine, in one person.

One of the finest elaborations of this truth came from Leo, the bishop of Rome. "The properties of each nature," he wrote to the council, "were preserved entire, and came together to form one person. Humility was assumed by majesty, weakness by strength, mortality by eternity; and to pay the debt that we incurred, an inviolable nature was united to a nature that can suffer . . . . The Lord of the universe allowed his infinite majesty to be overshadowed, and took upon him the form of a servant: The impassible God did not disdain to become passible, and the immortal one to be subject to the laws of death."

This classical, orthodox affirmation from Chalcedon made it possible to tell the story of Jesus as good news. Since Jesus was a normal human being, bone of our bone and flesh of our flesh, he could fulfill every demand of God's moral law, and he could suffer and die a real death. Since he was truly God, his death was able to satisfy divine justice. God himself had provided the sacrifice.

The difficulty with this Christology is its absolute uniqueness. According to normal human standards, it makes no sense. It doesn't add up. One human being plus one God does not equal one person, certainly not in any ordinary sense. But Christians do not claim that Jesus was ordinary.

In spite of all its difficulties, this view of Jesus enables us to speak about him and retain a real, fully human death, and simultaneously have it secure the necessary benefits for mankind. Christians hold that it provides an acceptable answer to the question, "Who is Jesus?"

The Worship of Christ

This witness to Jesus' unique role in God's plan of salvation is more than the brainchild of some Greek theologians assembled in solemn councils. It echoes from worshiping Christian congregations across the centuries and around the globe today. It resounds in the adoring praise of the church. "Out of the overflow of the heart the mouth speaks" (Matt. 12:34).

Richard Hooker, the Anglican divine, once said, "Our first eloquence concerning him is in our silence." But surely our second is in song. A deep instinct has always inspired the church to sing of the mystery of the incarnate Word. The living church is not so much a school of people holding all the correct doctrines; it is a worshiping congregation of God's people.

Open any Christian hymnbook and check the great hymns, phrase upon phrase, and the impact becomes unmistakable:

> O for a thousand tongues to sing
> My great Redeemer's praise,
> The glories of my God and King . . .

> Kyrie eleison,
> Christi eleison,
> Kyrie eleison, . . .

> Crown him the Lord of heaven,
> One with the Father known, . . .

> All hail, Redeemer, hail!
> For Thou hast died for me;
> Thy praise and glory shall not fail
> Throughout eternity.

The language demonstrates that Christian people maintain an attitude of mind, a spirit of submission, before Jesus Christ that can only be called worship. If Michelangelo were to enter our living room we would rise to meet him. But if Jesus Christ were to enter, we would fall down and worship him. He is more than a model or a teacher. He is God incarnate and reigning Lord.

Christians, today, are tempted to abandon this exclusive view of Jesus. Respect for other religions compels them to question the New Testament portrait of the Lord Jesus Christ. It seems more modest to speak of Christianity as "the religion of Western man." But that temptation is self-defeating. Such a view destroys the heart of the Christian faith. For the New Testament's universal Savior it substitutes a religion that Jesus and the apostles—as well as the orthodox believers of all ages—would criticize as quickly as they did alternative religions of their own times.

Students of world religions often compare true faith to a mountain peak. The trails to the top, they say, all start at the base of the mountain and wind their own ways to the summit, converging as they draw near the top. So those who climb the mountain come closer to each other the farther they climb. On the summit they all, at last, see the same God. Christians, however, insist that none has stood upon that summit except Jesus Christ.

10

The Agony and the Answer

C. S. Lewis's fantasy, *The Lion, the Witch, and the Wardrobe,* is a children's story. Four youngsters from England find themselves transported magically to the land of Narnia, a fascinating world where animals, such as fauns and beavers, talk and plan just like people. The creator of Narnia is Aslan, the great and powerful lion. But when the children arrive, Narnia is under the influence of a wicked White Witch.

One of the children, Edmund, turns against his brother and sisters and joins forces with the Witch. To save Edmund, Aslan gives himself to be killed in Edmund's place. He surrenders to the White Witch and her evil Hags. They bind him on a great Stone Table and slay him.

The next day Edmund's sisters, Susan and Lucy, look in disbelief at the empty Table and Aslan, alive and strong.

"But what does it all mean?" asks Susan, finally satisfied that Aslan is not a ghost.

"It means," Aslan explains, "that though the Witch knew the Deep Magic, there is a magic deeper still which she did not know. . . . If she could have looked a little further back, . . . she would have known that when a willing victim who had committed no treachery was killed in a traitor's stead, the Table would crack and Death itself would start working backwards." [1]

Death itself would start working backwards! That is the Christian faith. The death and resurrection of Jesus Christ have set in motion a process that runs counter to the direction of life around us.

"After desire has conceived," the Bible says, "it gives birth to sin; and sin, when it is full-grown, gives birth to death" (James 1:15). That is the downward course of mankind. But Christ has brought life and immortality to light through the gospel. And the cross on which Jesus died starts death working backwards.

The Crucifixion

It is possible to look at the cross from a purely historical perspective. Crucifixion was a common penalty for criminals in Roman times. The Persians probably introduced this shocking form of execution but the Romans seized the gruesome practice in order to rid themselves of terrorists, slaves, and hardened criminals.

The victim usually endured a merciless scourging with straps laced with thorns or jagged bits of bone. During the beating the soldiers charged with the execution often indulged their bestial emotions. Some victims died from the flogging alone. Jesus survived.

After the beating, the soldiers bound or nailed the victim to a rough beam, the horizontal log for the cross. Burdened with this he had to drag himself through the streets to the place of execution. There soldiers lifted the cross-beam, bearing the victim, above the earth and secured it to the vertical post. Finally, the soldiers nailed the feet to the cross. Time did the rest—fever, shock, thirst, pain, delirium, and death.

This was Jesus' destiny because he had inflamed the hatred of the Jewish authorities. His contempt of Jewish traditions and his claims of divine powers brought him at last to the Sanhedrin, the Jewish high court. These enraged men condemned him to death for blasphemy. According to the Mosaic law that meant death by stoning. Rome, however, did not grant the Jews the power to carry out executions. So the Jewish authorities whisked Jesus away to the Roman governor, Pontius Pilate.

"We caught this man misleading the people," they cried, "telling them not to pay taxes to the Emperor and claiming that he himself is the Messiah, a king."

In order to gain the death penalty, the religious authorities, while spiriting Jesus through the darkened city's streets, had shifted the charge against him. Before Pilate, Jesus was a rabble-rouser, a conspirator. The charge was high treason. Pilate tried to sidestep the death penalty, but under pressure he eventually crumbled and gave the order: "Crucify him." That is the story of the cross on one level.

There is, however, another level of meaning in these events, a level that the historian usually refuses to enter. We enter it, however, when we ask, what was God doing in these events? That is another matter. On the surface, the cross has all the signs of a judicial murder. But on another level of meaning—the level on which the Bible discusses it—the cross reveals an unbelievable gospel.

The Gospel of the Cross

I call it the gospel because it is astoundingly good news. The cross says men and women can now find forgiveness with God. Apart from the rescue mission of God we were like helpless sailors drifting aimlessly at sea in a leaking lifeboat. Our only hope was in the appearance of someone outside our little world. That is what the cross reveals. A rescue party has come from the Hidden World.

Basic to the Christian view of the cross, then, is a concept of God. As long as we think of God as some vague, distant force, we will never see the need for reconciliation between God and man. Or if we insist on a god who only loves, who knows neither holiness nor wrath, the cross will never make sense to us, not any Christian sense.

In that view we are asking God to be what we despise in men. The man who cannot express anger cannot truly love. The person who dismisses treachery or infidelity with a wave of the hand, as if it were nothing, cannot be a true friend or a true husband. That will never do. In God, love and holiness must somehow harmonize.

Surely, deep within us there lies a sense that all is not right with God and something ought to be done about it. Why do we make our resolutions? Why do we try to be better men and women? We sense that we are not what we ought to be. Sometimes we tell our analyst about it. Sometimes we try to atone for our failures and sins. Sometimes we deaden the pain with drugs.

This gulf between us and God is not merely an intellectual one, as though the right course on ethics or the right book on religion could fill it. No, the real gulf is in the spiritual realm. We are separated from God by sin in our lives. And that sin deserves God's wrath—and God's condemnation. If we refuse to hear of God's holiness, we will never understand Jesus Christ or his cross.

Evidently Jesus saw his whole life and ministry in terms of his end. The words he heard at his baptism, for example, are a key to his understanding of the Old Testament. As Jesus came up out of the water, he heard a voice: "You are my Son whom I love; with you I am well pleased."

"You are my Son" comes from the second Psalm. "With you I am well pleased" is an echo of Isaiah, chapter 42. Together in the mind of Jesus they indicate that he considered himself the fulfillment of Israel's hope for a Messiah, the prophetic Servant of the Lord.

But if Jesus saw his own mission in terms of these prophetic passages, what must he have thought when Isaiah 53 lay open before him? Did he also read, "Surely he hath borne our griefs, and carried our sorrows," and know that this was the reason he came into the world?

During long hours Jesus must have turned over and over in his mind the significance of the prophets' words for the days that lay ahead of him. Apparently from the beginning he had seen the end of the road and had counted the cost. He saw his approaching death as a bitter necessity. Messiahship meant taking up the cross.

Why else was he baptized by John? Though he was no transgressor, he was numbering himself with the transgressors. He was taking the burden of men's sins as though it were his own. A mother or father whose son has fallen into some shameful crime can understand. Because of their love for their child they too enter into the guilt of another. It is not their sin, but they feel the shame of it as though it were their own.

Jesus, however, did more than feel the pain and shame of human sin. He actually endured the punishment of it. He met the demands of justice. He removed every impediment to God's forgiveness.

In the New Testament the central purpose of the death of Christ is clear enough. "God was reconciling the world to himself in Christ, not counting men's sins against them" (2 Cor. 5:19). God and men were once estranged from one another. Men's sins had created a barrier between them and God. "Your iniquities," shouted the prophet, "have separated you from your God" (Isa. 59:2). But the cross removed that barrier. It restored sinful men to a holy God.

The term for this reconciliation is atonement. William Tyndale, the English Bible translator, was probably the first person to use the term. He wanted to stress that Christ's death made possible the "at-one-ment" of rebellious sinners and a holy God. That much is clear in the New Testament.

Views of the Atonement

Christians have often differed with each other over the detailed explanations of the atonement. Some of them have considered the death of Jesus a ransom paid to Satan to gain the release of men from Satan's power. Satan captured Jesus in death but was surprised to find at Jesus' resurrection that he got more than he could handle. This is the so-called ransom theory. Jesus' death was the ransom paid to Satan in order to release imprisoned sinners.

Other Christians have described the atonement in terms of a payment owed to God. Man's sin, they say, is the failure to give to God the honor he rightly deserves. Dishonor is sin. But since God is infinite, his honor takes on infinite proportions. Man's debt, then, is infinite. This is his dilemma. Man *must* pay God his due; but no man *can* pay God his due. Since only man must pay the debt and only God can pay the debt, what mankind needs is a God-man. That is why, in mercy, God sent Jesus to make satisfaction for sin. He paid the debt we owe to God. This is the satisfaction theory of the atonement.

Still other Christians explain reconciliation in terms of the effect of the cross upon men. The example of a suffering Jesus arouses within us a deep admiration of him. We find the meaning of sacrificial love when we see it demonstrated so graphically on the cross. We are moved by Jesus' example to love others who may at first appear to us as undeserving of the slightest favor. When we love as he loved, we are drawn to God. This is the so-called "moral influence" theory of the atonement.

The New Testament, however, offers no single theory of the atonement. Instead it presents a series of dramatic word pictures to magnify the significance of Jesus' death.

According to the New Testament, we were in hopeless debt and Jesus paid the debt for us (Luke 7:41–50).

We were slaves and Jesus came to the marketplace to redeem us from bondage (Eph. 1:7).

We were condemned criminals before the judgment seat of God and Jesus bore our penalty in order to set us free (Rom. 5:16).

We were unclean Gentiles, excluded by our defilement of sin from the presence of God in the temple, and Jesus gave himself as a sacrifice to consecrate for us a way to the throne of mercy (Eph. 2:13–14).

We were children in disgrace far from home and Jesus brought us back to the family circle (Eph. 2:18–19).

We were captives confined to the fortress of Satan and Jesus broke in to deliver us (Col. 2:15).

The terminology of the bank, the slave market, the law court, the temple, the home, and the battlefield is pressed into the service of the gospel in order to throw light on the atonement of Christ. The cross destroyed the barrier between man and God. That is the point.

> What Thou, my Lord, hast suffered
> Was all for sinners' gain;
> Mine, mine was the transgression,
> But Thine the deadly pain.
> —*O Sacred Head, Now Wounded*

In his little book *On Christian Truth,* Harry Blamires suggests that we think of the human race aboard a hijacked jet-liner flying through time. "God himself directed its takeoff from the divine control-tower. The initiator of all evil, whom we call the Devil, managed to get a boarding pass." When the plane reached its cruising altitude, the Devil produced his weapons, threatened the pilot, and took control of the aircraft and all its passengers.

Thus the plane hopped on fearfully through history from airport to airport till "it was caught on the tarmac at Jerusalem, an outpost of the Roman empire, in the reign of Tiberius Caesar, where the Son of God offered himself as sole hostage in exchange for passengers and crew."[2] The scene has become so common in recent years that it serves well to bring an old truth up to date.

This meaning of the cross was not at first self-evident. Its significance appeared only after the resurrection of Jesus. Jesus' resurrection from the grave is like the finishing touch of some great artist. In a painting, for example, a master may allow his full plan to remain hidden until the last stroke of his brush. Every brush mark suggests his meaning, but its fullness never appears until he is done. That last touch brings the significance to every detail of the picture. So it is with the resurrection. We do not understand Jesus, nor do we understand the cross until we see it in the light of the resurrection.

The Resurrection

To many people Jesus' resurrection is the most incredible claim of the Christian faith. It is not the kind of thing, they say, that happens in our world. They know that if someone rushed up to them and announced that some friend of theirs had died three days before and had been buried, but had appeared for breakfast that morning, they would be inclined to question the informer's sanity.

Christians, then, need to explain why they believe that Jesus actually passed through death to the Hidden World and returned for a time to talk about it. Belief in Jesus' resurrection rests on three pieces of evidence: the appearances of Jesus to his disciples, the empty tomb, and the subsequent history of the Christian church.

The Gospels indicate that Jesus appeared on many occasions and to a large number of people—five hundred on one occasion. The records assure us that some of these people were at first quite incredulous. They were not easily convinced. Even if these appearances were not genuine, we must still explain the accounts.

Some have suggested that the appearances of Christ after the resurrection were merely psychic phenomena. If that were so, we would expect the conviction that Jesus was alive to grow progressively less vivid once the disciples ceased to be "in touch" with the Hidden World. We would also expect the followers who had not seen the evidence to be as sceptical as third parties usually are when confronted with reports of communications from the dead.

Neither of these expectations, however, correspond with the facts. The conviction about the resurrection became even more settled once the appearances ceased, and those who had not seen the risen Christ were won to a living faith just as those who had seen. The early Christian witnesses of the resurrection spoke not so much of some past appearance of Christ as of their own experience with the living Savior.[3]

The only other possible explanation is that the empty tomb and the whole series of appearances was a gigantic hoax. But as G. B. Caird once asked, which of the disciples of Jesus, scattered and disillusioned on Good Friday, could by Easter Day have planned and executed so elaborate and so successful a deception? The most likely reception for such a trick would have been derisive laughter.

Are we really to believe that men will die for a hoax? How could a "hoax" deceive thousands of people, and be perpetuated for two thousand years? On the whole it seems easier to believe the testimony of Peter, John, and the rest than to accept either of these explanations.[4]

Evidence for the Resurrection

The decisive evidence for the resurrection, however, is the impact it had on the lives of flesh-and-blood people. On Good Friday, Peter was a broken man, overwhelmed with a sense of shame at having denied Jesus in his hour of crisis. Within a few weeks, however, we find him standing before the Jewish authorities declaring under threat of persecution that "salvation is found in no one else, for there is no other name under heaven given to men by which we must be saved" (Acts 4:12). Something happened in the interval to transform a coward into a hero.

At one point the disciples were meeting in a locked room for fear of the Jews. Then something happened to send them out across the world with a burning zeal that no hardship could quench. Paul was persecuting the church, and something happened to make him its greatest missionary. The history of Christianity is simply full of examples of similar transformations. Nothing less than the resurrection will explain them.

For the apostles, the resurrection of Jesus was the last stroke of God's brush, the final disclosure of God's presence and mission in the life of Jesus. What had been hidden from them in his lifetime was revealed to them in his death and resurrection.

As James Smart once pointed out, Jesus' death stripped the disciples of all false expectations about the Messiah, and his resurrection opened their eyes to what Jesus had been about from his first day among them. It revealed to them the climactic fulfillment of the purpose of God which bound all their past history together. They discovered that even the Old Testament spoke of a Messiah who, through death and resurrection, would inaugurate God's rule over stubbornly resistant men.[5]

The resurrection, then, was the final proof that Jesus had conquered man's last enemy—death. He had shown beyond any possible doubt that his saving victory was complete. Death had started working backward. To live again was no pious hope or wishful thought; it was a certainty.

11

The Blue-Collar Deity

During what may have been ancient Israel's greatest crisis of faith—the time of the exile—the prophet Ezekiel served as a pastor to his displaced people. The refugees in Babylon had the paralyzing feeling that they were the doomed heirs of the past. "Don't you believe it," said Ezekiel. "God has plans for you."

Ezekiel's response was based upon a vision God had given him. He found himself in a valley full of dry, bleached bones. Apparently, some army had fallen in battle—victims of a swift and successful ambush. Time, vultures, and the Near Eastern sun had done the rest. The last signs of life had dried in the summer heat.

"Son of man," Ezekiel heard, "can these bones live?"

"O Sovereign Lord," he responded, "you alone know."

"Prophesy!" the Voice said. "Say to these dry bones, 'Hear the word of the Lord! . . . I will make breath enter you, and you will come to life. . . . Then you will know that I am the Lord.' "

Ezekiel did as he was told. And the bones moved and came together. Flesh appeared on them and breath entered them. They came to life and stood on their feet. Then the Lord said, "O my people, I will put my Spirit in you and you will live, and I will settle you in your own land. Then you will know that I the Lord . . . have done it" (Ez. 37:1–14).

This expectation of a community renewed by the Spirit of the Lord, a community filled and governed by the living presence of God, flows out from Ezekiel into the future. Centuries later the Christian church came to see itself as the fulfillment of Ezekiel's prophecy.

The Person of the Holy Spirit

Who is the Holy Spirit? Christians confess that he is the third Person of the Trinity. They hold that the God revealed by Jesus Christ has three distinct ways of being God.

First, he is far beyond us. He is the mysterious Source of all things, visible and invisible. The greatness and the grandeur of his nature are reflected in his handiwork—the crashing waves upon a New England shore, the predictability of the stars in their courses, the marvel of an infant's birth. He is beyond all that he has made. We call him Creator—and Father.

Second, God is before us. Jesus Christ demonstrated that God could veil himself in human flesh. He came to Bethlehem in the weakness of human birth. He submitted to the pains and frustrations of human life and died, at last, the vilest of human deaths. Yet through those thirty years on earth, and especially through his resurrection from the dead, he succeeded in convincing his disciples that he was God. "God was in Christ," they preached. So he is before us. We call him Redeemer—the Son.

Third, God is within us. He is that life-giving Spirit who witnesses to humanity about the Truth of God and creates a unique community of twice-born people called the church. By the Holy Spirit, Jesus can be everywhere present today. He is no longer limited to the first century, to the Aramaic language, to the hills of Galilee, and to a prescientific view of the world. The risen Christ is freed from the limits of time and space to walk into every person's life. By the Spirit he moves freely through the centuries and across cultures making salvation available to all. We call that Presence the Holy Spirit.

How did Christians come to these convictions about the Spirit? They had the Old Testament Scriptures to guide them along a certain trail of thought, and they had the life and teachings of Jesus to point to the end of the trail—the Christian understanding of the life and ministry of the Holy Spirit.

The Spirit in the Old Testament

When the Old Testament speaks of *spirit,* it reflects one of the earliest ideas about human life found in many parts of the ancient world: Man's life is dependent upon breath. Even in sleep man continues to breathe. Doesn't the chest rise and fall? And when man dies, doesn't breath depart from the body? So breath means life.

Apparently reflecting this belief, the Old Testament word for spirit is *ruach,* which means breath, wind, or spirit. Genesis tells us how man was created: "The Lord God formed man from the dust of the ground and breathed into his nostrils the breath of life, and man became a living being" (Gen. 2:7). God had his Spirit, and so did man.

This fact raises an unavoidable question: What is the relation between man's spirit and God's Spirit? Some eastern religions teach that man's spirit is a tiny spark from the great fire of God, a beam from the cosmic light of God.

In the Old Testament, however, the spirit of man is never presented as some sort of fragment of the Spirit of God. Neither do man's spirit and God's Spirit participate in some sort of cosmic life. Man, like all other living things, is always dependent upon God for life. But unlike other creatures, man's spirit enables him to have a personal relationship with God. Man can know God, love God, and serve God. His spirit is special. It makes his free and conscious commitment to God possible; it offers man the chance for personal contact with God.

Since the entrance of sin, however, man cannot know this relationship apart from God's special help. Sin turned man's freedom *for* God to a freedom *from* God. Man finds it impossible to reverse this change. Only as the Spirit of God subdues man's spirit, making him willing to confess his sin and his need of God's forgiveness, does he know again the freedom for God.

This is the work of God's Spirit throughout the Old Testament. Time and again he comes upon men to advance the Lord's saving purpose. He is the hidden power behind Joseph's wisdom in Egypt, behind the skill of Bezalel in designing the Tabernacle, behind the faithfulness of Caleb, behind the awe-inspiring feats of the judges, and the inspiration of the prophets. In time the *ruach* of God comes to stand for the work of the righteous and merciful God of Israel. He is no pervasive force in the universe; he is the invasive power in Israel. The idea is not immanence, but action. The Spirit of God is the Lord God in working clothes.

In the latter parts of the Old Testament this active power of God is a sure sign of God's presence. God's presence and God's Spirit are essentially the same thing. That is why the psalmist prayed, "Do not cast me from your presence," and immediately followed with the parallel clause, "or take your Holy Spirit from me" (Ps. 51:11).

When we reach the prophets we feel a fresh breeze. Some of these seers—like Ezekiel—look beyond the invasion and ruin of Israel and see another day, a coming age when God will no longer give his Spirit only to judges, priests, and prophets. He will pour out his Spirit upon everyone. As the prophet Joel put it:

> Your sons and daughters will prophesy,
> your old men will dream dreams,
> your young men will see visions.
> (Joel 2:28)

In a similar way, Jeremiah promised a day when a new covenant of the Spirit would be written on the human heart. Men would no longer live under the promptings of the Law; they would have the inner direction of the Spirit of God.

This coming age of the Spirit, forecast by the prophets, centered in a Leader who would be able to say:

> The Spirit of the Sovereign Lord is on me,
> because the Lord has anointed me
> to preach good news to the poor.

He has sent me to bind up the brokenhearted,
to proclaim freedom for the captives
and release for the prisoners.

(Isa. 61:1)

The Old Testament, then, leaves us leaning forward, looking for a brighter day when the Spirit will move beyond Israel to liberate hosts of other people—even Gentiles—through the Anointed One, the Messiah.

Jesus and the Spirit

When the reader opens the New Testament he is struck immediately by the fact that the Christian Gospels consider Jesus of Nazareth more than just another prophet in Israel. The Spirit descended upon those ancient voices only now and then. In Jesus Christ, the Spirit of God lives in his fullness. The birth narratives in Matthew and Luke trace Jesus' conception to the power of the Spirit. These nativity scenes are apparently painted to show that Jesus' life was a direct creation of the Spirit.

It naturally follows that when he opened his public ministry by his baptism at the hands of John the Baptist, the Spirit descended upon Jesus, and as John's Gospel says, "remained on him" (1:32). He received the Spirit "without limit." From that time on the Spirit was united to Jesus. He had, as it were, no mission apart from Jesus.

That is apparently the meaning of Jesus' later invitation in the Temple court: "If a man is thirsty, let him come to me and drink. Whoever believes in me, as the Scripture has said, "streams of living water will flow from within him." As the Gospel explains, he was speaking of the Spirit who would in time be given to all who believed. "Up to that time the Spirit had not been given, since Jesus had not yet been glorified" (John 7:37–39).

Time and again the Gospels trace Jesus' victories over hostile forces—demons, sickness and death—to the Spirit. That is why Jesus says, "If I drive out demons by the Spirit of God, then the kingdom of God has come upon you" (Matt. 12:28). The Spirit of God is the hidden explanation of Jesus' life.

Perhaps Peter in Cornelius's house gave the best summary when he explained: "God anointed Jesus of Nazareth with the Holy Spirit and power, and . . . he went around doing good and healing all who were under the power of the devil, because God was with him" (Acts 10:38).

In the New Testament, then, Jesus Christ is clearly the recipient and the bearer of the Holy Spirit. Men do not come to know the Spirit except through him.

But what about the great day of that Spirit which Ezekiel promised? When did those dry bones come together and take flesh and receive the breath of God? That came only after Jesus was "glorified"—after his death on Calvary and his resurrection from the grave. Christians call it Pentecost.

Pentecost

Pentecost was first a Jewish festival. It came seven weeks after the Passover, during which Jesus was crucified. Excitement among the pilgrims in Jerusalem was running high. During the festival about 120 disciples of Jesus were meeting in a home when an unusual thing happened. God's Spirit suddenly fell upon those gathered there. Some thought that it was a violent wind rushing through the house; others testified to tonguelike flames of fire resting on each of them.

Swept up in the experience, the disciples rushed into the streets and headed for the temple. Many of the visitors in the city saw them and followed because they heard their native tongue coming from the lips of the disciples.

Once at the temple Peter stood before the huge crowd and told them that the miracle they were witnessing was a fulfillment of the prophet Joel's promise about the outpouring of God's Spirit in the "last days." The explanation for the marvel, he said, lay in the recent crucifixion of Jesus of Nazareth. God had made him Lord and Messiah by raising him from the dead!

Peter's announcement of the resurrection was an astounding development. How could he ever substantiate such a claim? He appealed to the Jewish Scriptures which said that the Messiah would not be abandoned in death but would be enthroned at God's right hand, the position of authority and honor, until universal victory was his (Psalm 16:10 and 110:1).

But what do such Scriptures have to do with Jesus of Nazareth? He was the Messiah, said Peter. We know it is so, because " . . . God has raised this Jesus to life, and we are all witnesses of the fact" (Acts 2:32).

From the beginning, the apostles preached the resurrection of Jesus as the fulfillment of God's purpose announced in the Old Testament. Once crucified, the Messiah was exalted above the universe. Apart from that miracle, said the apostles, there is no gospel, no salvation, and no church. It is true. Therefore, "Repent," Peter told the Pentecost pilgrims, "and be baptized . . . in the name of Jesus Christ so that your sins may be forgiven. And you will receive the gift of the Holy Spirit" (Acts 2:38).

The Mission of the Spirit

Since that moment the Spirit has been at work in the church bearing witness to Christ, making men and women alive to God, enlightening the minds of believers, and changing them into the likeness of Christ. The Spirit's specific mission is to empower God's liberating forces launched by the appearance of Jesus Christ.

Through the Spirit the mission of Jesus assumed universal proportions. It spread from Palestine throughout the whole world, from the first century to all ages. The link between the historic appearance of Jesus and the universal ministry of the Holy Spirit is so close that the apostle Paul can say, "The Lord is the Spirit" (2 Cor. 3:17).

We need not suppose that Paul intended an absolute identification between Christ and the Spirit. He still spoke of Christ as a person who once lived at Nazareth but now lives in the Hidden World. What he apparently intended was an identity of purpose between Christ and the Spirit in their work of reconciliation. Both possess the same divine energy at work in Christian believers, renewing their inner life and leading them toward that day when even their spiritual bodies will reflect the glory and incorruptibility of Christ's resurrection body (Rom. 8:11).

Today many people think of the Spirit of God as a kind of detached spiritual essence scattered throughout humanity, working here and there quite apart from Jesus Christ who redeemed us. That is not the view of the New Testament. The first Christians believed that the Holy Spirit came to us from the Hidden World to reveal the Father Almighty who delivers us from spiritual slavery through Jesus Christ and offers us life in a new dimension. They knew the Spirit not as an alternative to, but as a manifestation of the presence of Christ.

The presence of the Spirit, then, does not displace the presence of Christ. That can never happen in the Christian faith. True faith must always center in Christ through whom God reconciled the world unto himself. It is the Holy Spirit who makes God personal to each of us by uniting us to Christ. He is that breath from God who makes our dry bones live.

12

Whispers of the Wind

In evangelical Christianity one of the popular stories from the life of Jesus tells how Nicodemus, a member of the Jewish ruling council, came to Jesus one night and said to him, "Rabbi, we know you are a teacher who has come from God. For no one could perform the miraculous signs you are doing if God were not with him."

"I tell you the truth," said Jesus, "unless a man is born again, he cannot see the kingdom of God."

Nicodemus hardly knew what to say. He had never heard of a second birth. "How," he asked, "can a man be born when he is old?"

"Flesh gives birth to flesh," Jesus explained, "but the Spirit gives birth to spirit. . . . The winds blows wherever it pleases. You hear its sound, but you cannot tell where it comes from or where it is going. So it is with everyone born of the Spirit" (John 3:1–8).

It is one of those fascinating exchanges from the life of Jesus. Christians have often wondered why Nicodemus, a respected religious leader, knew so little about the Holy Spirit. Apparently he had never heard of the new birth and wasn't sure what to make of Jesus. His problem is worth pursuing. What does the Spirit of God do in the world?

Jesus' comparison—the wind and the Spirit—is a helpful starting point. It contains a significant reminder: God's ways are not man's ways. The Spirit's plans are not open to all. Men can see the effects of his work, but no one can infallibly explain just how or where he moves. When men have dared to claim control over the Spirit of God, saying he is here or he is there, they have usually proved themselves fools.

> Oh, the depth of the riches of the wisdom
> and knowledge of God!
> How unsearchable his judgments,
> and his paths beyond tracing out!
> (Rom. 11:33)

We only dare to raise the question of the Spirit's work because the Bible itself raises it and the Christian faith rests upon it. God seems to invite us to listen intently for the whispers of the Wind.

The Spirit in Creation

When Christians confess their faith in the Holy Spirit through the Nicene Creed they refer to him as "the Lord and Giver of life." As we have seen, the link between the Spirit and the breath of life is basic. But what is life? One after another of the mysteries of the universe have yielded to the relentless investigations of the human mind, yet this question remains unanswered. We can recognize life, we can nurture life, and we can destroy life, but we cannot explain life.

The creed's conviction that life comes from the Spirit can be traced to Jesus Christ, who once said to his disciples: "The Spirit gives life; the flesh counts for nothing" (John 6:63). What did Jesus mean? What life does the Spirit give? Is he the source of all natural life? Or is he the giver of eternal life to those who believe? Christians believe that he is both. Like the wind, he moves mysteriously through the natural world and through the spiritual realms.

The Bible portrays the Spirit as the energizing power in creation. "In the beginning," we read in the first verse of Genesis, "God created the heavens and the earth. Now the earth was formless and empty, darkness was over the surface of the deep, and the Spirit of God was hovering over the waters" (1:1–2).

The image of the hovering Spirit is a striking picture. It recalls the mother bird with outstretched wings hovering over her young to cherish and protect them. The figure implies that the earth held the germs of life within it and that the Holy Spirit caused this life to spring forth so that he might lead that life to its intended destiny.

The Spirit of God appears a second time in the creation story when the Lord God makes man "from the dust of the ground." He formed man and "breathed into his nostrils the breath of life, and man became a living human being" (Gen. 2:7). The Hebrews apparently believed that the Spirit, this outgoing breath of God, was the source of life. Job, for example, said, "The Spirit of God has made me; the breath of the Almighty gives me life" (Job 33:4).

These references to the Spirit's activity in creation strongly suggest that he is present in the cosmic process at all levels, but in a special way in human life. Man can only find his true life as he fulfills his destiny. He was created to have personal communion with God—and the Holy Spirit makes that possible. The apostle Paul reminded the Athenians of this when he told them "the God who made the world and everything in it . . . gives all men life and breath and everything else" (Acts 17:24–25). This is the reason Christians hold that life itself is a sacred gift of God.

The Witness of the Spirit

What is the connection between the human spirit and the Holy Spirit? In the early days of Christianity as the gospel spread beyond the limits of Judaism and entered the world of Greek culture, many Christians accepted the idea that the human spirit reflects the Holy Spirit in a special way. Irenaeus, the pastor of the church at Lyons, for example, argued, "The Word bestows

the Spirit in all . . . on some by way of creation . . . ; on some
by way of adoption." But this notion goes too far.

As Jesus suggested in his conversation with Nicodemus, sin
has distorted the natural harmony that once existed between
flesh—natural man—and Spirit—the life of God. Natural communion is now impossible between flesh and Spirit. Man must
be made alive by the Spirit if he is to see the kingdom of God.

The original likeness to God's Spirit in the human spirit is
not totally lost, however; some hint of the created purpose remains
in man. It helps to explain mankind's sense of right and wrong.
All men, except the pathological, seem to feel guilty when they
transgress some standard of morality. Specific sins seem to vary
from culture to culture, but no tribe or society endures with
total lawlessness. This conscience, as we call it, may be a clue
to the life from the Spirit.

Christians have also traced mankind's love of the truth, displays
of creativity, and acts of generosity to the Spirit of God. Like
James they hold that "every good and perfect gift is from above,
coming down from the Father of heavenly lights, who does not
change like shifting shadows" (James 1:17). In this sense, the
scientist, the painter, and the humanitarian are working with
God as they make truth and beauty and goodness their goals.
Christian theologians call it "common grace," meaning that the
gifts of God are not limited to Christian people, but come through
all men.

Perhaps, however, the supreme instance of the Spirit's ministry
to all mankind is the almost universal, religious question of people.
Over the centuries and throughout the world men and women
have tried to get into touch with the universal and the eternal.
Man is a compulsive worshiper. This spiritual longing is distinctive to man. This sets him apart from all other creatures. He
seems to be permanently maladjusted to his environment, always
searching for the Hidden World. Why? Christians believe that
this restlessness at the center of human existence is a faint whisper
of the Holy Spirit inviting men and women to find life in Christ.

Since the appearance of God in flesh, the Holy Spirit often
confronts men and women directly—on the basis of the apostolic

witness to the incarnation. He impresses them with their need to change, to be different people. That is his specific mission in preparation for a presentation of the gospel.

This is the mission Jesus stressed as he was leaving his disciples. "It is for your good that I am going away," he told them. "Unless I go away, the Counselor will not come to you; but if I go, I will send him to you. When he comes, he will convict the world of guilt in regard to sin and righteousness and judgment" (John 16:7-8). He proves men wrong about their ideas of a benevolent God who tolerates sin; wrong about their conceptions of righteousness achieved apart from Christ; wrong about their impressions of judgment ignoring the decisive place of the cross in God's eyes. All this is the Spirit's mission in the world.

The title Jesus gave the Spirit—"the Counselor"—is in Greek, the *Paraclete.* This literally means the one who stands alongside. It is a title early Christians also used when speaking of Christ. He has come to stand by the believer's side, to speak in his defense, to uphold him when his knees begin to buckle. It is a vivid image of his work for us. But it is also his image of the Spirit's work. He is the other Counselor, the Voice at our side speaking of Christ.

In Washington, D.C., the Speaker of the House of Representatives has a parliamentary assistant who stands by constantly. He anticipates the business of the House, the decisions to be made, and the procedures to be followed. He is always ready to give counsel and direction. He is the *paraclete,* the one who stands by, an apt image of the Holy Spirit.

The Spirit in the Church

We might approach the second area of the Spirit's ministry through a picture drawn from today's urban world. The loneliness and isolation in contemporary urban societies can be illustrated by a ride in an elevator in an apartment building. You know the people around you are your neighbors, but you have no idea who they are. You glance around quickly, trying not to stare at anyone. You see the other riders but you do not speak. You are crowded together for a few brief moments, but there is no community. Finally, as the doors open upon the seventh floor, you are freed from the silent embarrassment. This is a portrait of what sociologist David Riesman once called *The Lonely Crowd*.

The second ministry of the Holy Spirit addresses that need. He has come to create Christian community. The New Testament term for it is *koinonia*. It is the common life of Christ shared by the whole church; it is the fellowship of the Spirit.

We can find a vivid description of this Christian community in the Bible just after the account of the Spirit's appearance at Pentecost. The Book of Acts tells us that the earliest believers "devoted themselves to the apostles' teaching and to the fellowship, to the breaking of bread and to prayer. . . . All the believers were together and had everything in common. . . . They broke bread in their homes and ate together with glad and sincere hearts, praising God and enjoying the favor of all the people" (Acts 2:42–47).

At Pentecost a new and vital corporate life entered upon the stage of history, a new spiritual community based upon common beliefs, mutual trust, and, above all, life in the Spirit. Jesus Christ made it possible and the Holy Spirit made it work. The Spirit was so real to these first Christians that they considered him the invisible leader of their community.

For example, in their report to the scattered churches after one conference, the disciples explained that they reached their decision because it "seemed good to the Holy Spirit and to us" (Acts 15:28). This was more than empty religious prattle. They believed deeply in their unseen companion. The apostle Paul reflected the same awareness of the Spirit's presence in his prayer for the "fellowship of the Holy Spirit" (2 Cor. 13:14).

This creation of a united spiritual community was the primary purpose in the Holy Spirit's descent on the day of Pentecost. The Lord led Israel out of slavery in Egypt, through the desert, to the foot of Mount Sinai to establish his covenant with them and constitute them "the people of God." Likewise, at Pentecost the Holy Spirit took the good news of Jesus' death and resurrection and created the new covenant; he formed the new "people of God."

This spiritual oneness is more than a creedal statement; it is the heart of Christian reality. Professor J. A. Findlay once suggested that in Jesus' parable of the Pharisee and the Publican, the Pharisee was probably repeating the familiar Jewish prayer: "God, I thank you that I was not born a Gentile, but a Jew: not a slave, but a free man: not a woman, but a man." And, Findlay continued, when Paul wrote, "In Christ there is neither Jew nor Greek, neither slave nor free, neither male nor female" he was deliberately contradicting each phrase of the prayer which he had been taught to pray in his childhood. "Something," said Findlay, "had happened to a man who can do this."[1]

Regeneration

Just what does happen to a person who receives the new life of the Spirit? What is the Spirit's ministry to a Christian believer?

According to the New Testament, the work of God in the gospel includes the objective events of Jesus' life and the subjective gifts of the Spirit's mission. Both are essential for salvation. We have already considered Christ's reconciling work for spiritual rebels. It is time now to trace the outline of the Spirit's work in believers.

The initial work of the Spirit in the Christian is the new birth that Jesus revealed to Nicodemus. Theologians call it "regeneration." The apostle Paul once called it the "new creation." It is that work of the Spirit which transforms a spiritually lifeless person into a child of God. It is the personal experience of Ezekiel's resurrected dry bones. In this regeneration no one receives another ego. The transformed individual is the same person. All his basic parts remain intact—only after the Spirit's work, the person is alive to God.

Perhaps the best illustration of the new birth is found in the orchard. The successful grafting of a shoot of a cultivated apple tree upon the stock of a wild tree results in choice fruit on the once wild tree. Without the graft the wild tree is incapable of bearing fruit worth eating. But let the gardener graft this tiny shoot upon the wild stock and in time he will find luscious apples. Somehow the little graft has the remarkable power to convert the sap and the vital forces into something good.

We are all wild trees incapable of producing acceptable fruit. The Holy Spirit, however, grafts into all who trust in Christ something that they lack by nature. Then good things happen.

Sanctification

The second ministry of the Spirit in the believer involves those good things. Theologians call this "sanctification." It is the Spirit's mysterious life transforming the Christian into the likeness of Christ, producing in him all those virtues that remind others of Jesus Christ. Paul once called them "the fruit of the Spirit." He had in mind such things as love, joy, peace, patience, kindness, goodness, faithfulness, gentleness, and self-control (Gal. 5:22–23). These are the signs of sanctification.

If a court of law required evidence that a man were cruel, a prosecuting attorney would only have to produce the man's battered wife or his abused daughter. The convincing evidence would lie in the external acts. Just so, the life arising from the Holy Spirit is evident when the ego is gone from the center of life, when the selfish possessiveness of a man has been curbed and his dominant thought is changed from "What do I get out of it?" to "What can I do for Christ and others?"

This life from the Spirit is unique. We cannot equate it with any form of law-keeping, but neither can the true Christian use the Spirit as an excuse for lawlessness. Any identification of life by the Spirit with obedience to rules and regulations leads to a terrible perversion. Such a link suggests that the Christian faith is something external, something that can be found in actions alone. And that is simply untrue. Such an attitude is only a step away from considering faith a matter of bookkeeping.

The simplicity of such a view gives it a certain attractiveness. You open an account with God. On the credit side you enter all the good things you do: attend church regularly, contribute to worthy charities, raise your children to respect the law. There are, of course, entries on the other side of the ledger: the theft of office equipment, the unreported income on the tax form, the little affair on the business trip. The goal of this conception of religion is to total both sides of the account and have the credits exceed the debits.

The disastrous mistake in all this is the belief that a decent person can earn God's favor. All sorts of evils result from this perverted scheme: self-righteousness, contempt for others, spiritual blindness.

The only escape from it is through the Holy Spirit. He convinces us that we have our religion all wrong. The Christian faith does not consist of feverish attempts to earn God's favor by being good. It consists of humble acceptance of God's mercy arising from Christ's goodness. What we need more than anything else is God's forgiveness—and we can have it if we will wholeheartedly believe that Christ's death and resurrection removed every barrier to our reconciliation with God. This reversal in thinking, however, is so radical that men and women do not achieve it without the help of the Holy Spirit.

Even at the point of accepting the gospel lies another danger. No sooner do people reject the "bookkeeping" plan of salvation than they are confronted by an equally dangerous alternative. The promise of freedom from "bookkeeping" religion opens up the possibility of abuse of Christian freedom.

When told that they are free from the yoke of religious regulations, some people jump to the conclusion that they are free from any master at all. The apostle Paul discovered how often Christian converts exchange the bondage of self-righteousness for the slavery to self-expression. And it was he who spoke of "the law of the Spirit of life in Christ Jesus" (Rom. 8:2).

Life in the Spirit, he said, is more than a sense of release from the slavery to sin and death; it is also a new personal passion and inward power to please the One who frees us. That is the reality of the new birth which eluded Nicodemus before his significant conversation with Jesus.

13

God in Three Persons

The maps of the early explorers of America always included vast unexplored territories. Courageous seamen had touched the shorelines of the continent. What they had touched was real. But their maps reveal that they knew almost nothing about the uncharted wilderness of the interior.

The same is true when Christians speak of the inner life of God. They know that God revealed something of himself in his covenant with Israel, in the life, death, and resurrection of Jesus Christ, and in the surprising appearance of the Holy Spirit at Pentecost. This disclosure of God recorded in Scripture, like the continental shoreline, is real, but where does it lead? What does it suggest about the interior life of God? The doctrine of the Trinity is the church's attempt to trace something of that reality.

The Christian creeds, guided by that shoreline revealed in Scripture, help to plot the way to the life of God. But, as Christians have always acknowledged, so much terrain remains a mystery. The doctrine of the Trinity is so difficult to understand because no other teaching of the church carries us so deeply into the nature of God himself. It is like plunging into the impenetrable forests of an uncharted continent.

Christians, however, encouraged by the clues along the shoreline, do not fear the unknown. On the contrary, as they look to God, their first response is not dread but praise. That is why they sing with George W. Frazer:

Father, Son, and Holy Spirit—
Three in one! we give thee praise
For the riches we inherit,
Heart and voice to Thee we raise!
We adore Thee! we adore Thee!
Thee we bless, thro' endless days!
—*God, Our Father, We Adore Thee*

What, then, do Christians mean when they sing of "three in one"? While affirming their belief in one God, Christians confess that the one true God has revealed himself as Father, Son, and Holy Spirit.

To many people such a statement is sheer nonsense. It is utter foolishness to say God is both one and three. And even Christians themselves are often hard pressed to explain what they mean when they sing of the "blessed Trinity." They often appeal to the mysteries of their faith and make no attempt to spell out what they mean by this central doctrine of their religion.

Neither response should surprise us. Since God is who he is, Christians will always have to live with the mystery of the Trinity. When we ask about life in the Hidden World, we are probing both the ultimate reality of the visible universe and the baffling depths of personal existence. Both astrophysicists and psychiatrists freely confess their wonder before the unknown in outer and inner space. In fact, every area of serious study has its frontiers of knowledge where the known meets the unknown. Why should the Christian faith apologize for its mysteries?

The Experience of the Trinity

The first approach, then, to the wonder of the holy Trinity is not in a naive question of mathematics: one or three? After all, Christians have never confessed God's unity and his plurality in the same sense. They came to faith in the holy Trinity, not through mathematics but through revelation and experience. They could not testify of what God had done for them and to them in any way other than through the doctrine of the Trinity.

Israel's faith focused upon God the Creator of all things, the Lord of heaven and earth, who revealed himself to Israel by his great redeeming acts. He delivered the enslaved people of Israel from Egypt; he led them through their wilderness journey; he gave them a land of their own; he sent them prophets and kings. And through all these events Israel came to worship the Lord as a God of righteousness and grace. Even when the nation faced ruin in the face of foreign invaders, a remnant in Israel saw that the Lord was somehow working out his purpose for his people.

This faith in a God who is the Father Almighty passed on to Christianity primarily because it was the faith Jesus taught and demonstrated to his disciples. The disciples saw, however, that Jesus was himself an inextricable part of that faith. When they tried to explain what Jesus meant to them they found no adequate word except the word "Lord."

By identifying Jesus with Jahweh, the Lord of the Old Testament, early Christians fully knew what an incredible claim they were making. Yet they gladly faced the ridicule that followed the claim. They could not escape the impact of Jesus upon them and the compelling evidence they found of his deity, primarily his resurrection from the grave. He held the keys of death and hell. So to be truthful about Jesus of Nazareth they announced in Jerusalem that he was in fact God. The Lord had come to earth in human flesh.

The first Christians also said they experienced an indwelling Presence, a power not their own. When he was with them, Jesus had promised to send to them—after his death and resurrection—his Spirit. And so it happened.

As we have seen, fifty days after Jesus' resurrection the disciples experienced in Jerusalem an overwhelming event—wind and fire and tongues! All who spoke in this supernatural power interpreted it to mean the fulfillment of Jesus' promise. His Spirit—the Father's Spirit—had come to fill them and empower them to be witnesses of God's work for them and in them.

This was more than an exalted spiritual or mystic mood of the soul. This was God's Spirit sweeping into man's spirit. It was the birth of the church, the community of God. The Lord of the exodus and Sinai, the same divine Person who gave the

Law and sent the Sacrifice, had come to create a new community of faith.

These three realities, then—the Father Almighty, the incarnate Word, the empowering Holy Spirit—were more than a mathematical riddle or a doctrine propounded by theologians. They were a single personal reality in the lives of Christians, a single relationship to the one God as Father, revealed in Christ, and made real through the Spirit.

The first Christians professed this faith as they were baptized in the name of the Father, Son, and Holy Spirit (Matt. 28:17–21), and as they sought the benediction of heaven through "the grace of the Lord Jesus Christ and the love of God and the fellowship of the Holy Spirit" (2 Cor. 13:14).

Such plurality in unity is often a mark of creative genius. The *Unfinished Symphony* first existed in the mind of Schubert; it then became incarnate in a score written on paper and in sounds produced by instruments; then it became a spirit, so that a music lover in New Zealand can write to a music lover in Sweden and ask—without any need to play the music for confirmation—how and why the third movement was never written.[1]

Anyone who tries to dismiss the Trinity as an antiquated theological riddle is dismissing the Christian God—and with him the Christian faith. This doctrine is the foundation of the Christian life. We cannot enter into the full meaning of God as he was revealed to the first Christians unless we enter into the meaning of the God who is revealed as Father, Son, and Holy Spirit.

Across the centuries Christians have claimed that God as Holy Trinity fits their own actual experience of God. Take prayer, for example. The Christian believer comes to God the Father. That is the characteristic movement of prayer. But he comes to God "through Jesus Christ our Lord." Christ is not only God's means of approaching us; he is also our door of access to the Father. Finally, if the Christian prays at all he prays "in the Spirit." The life from God that enables the Christian to come to God is the Holy Spirit. Father, Son, and Spirit, then, are realities of the life of prayer, yet we know that it is the one God we meet in the experience of prayer.

The Doctrine of the Trinity

For a century or so after the ministry of Jesus, Christians did not put their new experience of God into explanatory words. As Oxford theologian Leonard Hodgson once put it: Christianity was a Trinitarian religion before it had a Trinitarian theology. The doctrine of the Trinity was the theology required by the Trinitarian faith. The earliest Christians, like the Jews before them, intended to remain strict monotheists, but they also worshiped Jesus and exulted in the presence of the Holy Spirit—just as men through the ages enjoyed light without ever bothering to explain it.

Even the earliest Trinitarian expressions of the Christian faith prevented Christianity from falling under the influence of either pantheistic or deistic religions. A faith in God which is at the same time faith in Jesus Christ as Lord can never be pantheistic because Jesus Christ claimed to be the exclusive truth and life of God. He revealed God to mankind at a particular time through a particular life. In a similar way, a faith in God which is also a faith in the Holy Spirit cannot become deistic because it is through the Holy Spirit that Almighty God acts directly, and at times miraculously, in the affairs of men.

When early Christians first tried to explain their Trinitarian faith in terms that outsiders could understand, they often resorted to two basic explanations. These two different tracks reach the same fundamental point: the absolute unity and uniqueness of God. We call one *subordinationism* and the other *monarchianism*. Both proved to have major weaknesses as enduring explanations of Trinitarian reality, but both moved the church toward greater clarity in its faith.

Subordinationism

Greek religious philosophy often explained reality in terms of a supreme Mind—a transcendent First Principle. Under this sovereign Ruler there was a hierarchy of divine beings who acted as intermediaries between the supreme Mind and the physical world. These divine beings served as a cosmic ladder stretching from the changeless realm to the material universe. Divinity was a matter of degree. Thus, one could speak of a plurality of divine beings while retaining an ultimate unity in reality.

In such a setting it was tempting for Christians to describe the Trinity by appealing to these Greek ideas acknowledging the supreme Power and his subordinate divine beings. But this temptation was dangerous. It suggested that when the New Testament spoke of "Father, Son, and Holy Spirit" it meant the "ultimate God and two intermediaries." Why should the God of the Bible, the God of Creation and Sinai and Calvary, need intermediaries? Is he somehow banned from his own creation?

Furthermore, what can we mean if we say Jesus Christ is divine, but at the same time say that he is not in the fullest sense God? Are we to believe that Jesus Christ, worshiped as Lord ever since his resurrection, was only some envoy of the true God? Clearly subordinationism wanted to avoid any hint of three gods (tritheism), but in adopting the traditional Greek idea of intermediaries it had introduced another set of unacceptable ideas about the Trinity.

The most troubling case for subordinationism came early in the fourth century from a popular minister in Alexandria, Egypt. Arius felt that his bishop had overstressed the unity of God. To set the record straight Arius started preaching about the differences between the Father and the divine Logos (the Word). He turned to the Greek idea of the God beyond existence, who is the one source of all things.

Arius interpreted the Word, who assumed flesh, as a creature different in essence from God the Father. He is unlike any other creature; he is "before times and before ages." He is divine and unique. And yet "there was a time when he was not." He does not share God the Father's uncreated existence.

Arius apparently had a knack for public relations and encouraged his followers to turn out catchy jingles setting his doctrine to bawdy tunes for barbershop harmony.

If you want the Logos-doctrine,
  I can serve it hot and hot—
God begot him and before he was begotten,
  he was not.

Before this distortion of the Holy Trinity could be suppressed, the emperor, Constantine, had to convene a general council of the church. Hundreds of church leaders had to debate the pros and cons for two generations.

Monarchianism

The sharp alternative to subordinationism in the early church was monarchianism. The name comes from the attempt to retain a faith in one holy Monarch of all creation. Christians who attempted to explain the Trinity in this way saw the weaknesses of subordinationism. So they asked, why not dispense with any real distinctions in the Trinity? Why not say that the Trinity is the one indivisible God?

When asked to explain the expressions Father, Son, and Holy Spirit, the monarchists responded that these are merely different ways in which God is seen by human beings. They may be different designations of his attributes, much as the sun is bright and hot and round, or they may be three appearances of the one God—first as Father, then as Son, and now as Spirit. But in either case, they do not refer to any true distinctions within the supreme Monarch.

Three in One

Perceptive Christians, however, saw that this view of God was seriously deficient in describing the revelation of God recorded in the Bible. The designations Father, Son, and Holy Spirit do in fact refer to something real within God.

To identify these distinctions, the church used the Greek term *hypostases* and its Latin counterpart *personae*. Our English word *persons* comes from the Latin. Whether in Greek or Latin, the early Christians intended to designate something genuinely three-fold when they spoke of Father, Son, and Holy Spirit. They knew that the Trinity is more than three attributes or three appearances of God. Within his own mysterious being God *is* Father, Son, and Holy Spirit. The designations are just ways in which God is God. Within the Godhead there are three "persons" who are neither three Gods nor three parts of God, but coequally and coeternally God.

The trouble with our English word *person* is its connotation of "personality." It carries the idea of an individual center of conscious life and independent activity. So three "persons" suggests to us Tom, Dick, and Harry. Such an idea is obviously inappropriate of God. But early Christians speaking either Greek or Latin never intended these ideas when they spoke of God "in three persons."

What early Christians wanted to affirm were the actual distinctions within the Godhead—the bearers of the differing relations within the one Almighty God. "Person," applied to God, meant a genuine and self-supported presentation of the reality of God.

While Christians knew that the names, Father, Son or Logos, and Spirit were analogies of God's inherent life, they believed that the names corresponded to what God was really like. Some actual distinctiveness was behind the titles Father, Son, and Spirit. And that distinctiveness was not three gods, but a trinity within the one personal God.

In summary, the Father is God, the Son is God, and the Spirit is God. The result is not three gods, but one. What they share equally and completely is deity. At the same time, the Father is not the Son, the Son is not the Spirit, and the Spirit is not the Father. The distinctions are real. The "Persons," then, are within the one personal deity.

Beyond that summation perhaps the best Christian response is praise in song—precisely what we find in the churches. After all, genuine love always moves beyond descriptions to the wonder of acceptance.

14

New People

"The organized church doesn't have much to offer me anymore," said one thoughtful critic. "In my opinion, the institutional conglomerate we call the church today is not the church that was ordained by God . . . . It seems the modern church in America long ago cut its ties to that God-ordained foundation and has been drifting with the cultural current ever since." [1]

To support his charge Mike Yaconelli pointed to the churches' costly buildings, their professional leaders, and their in-grown meetings. He was too close to the truth to make any conscientious Christian comfortable.

The charges are real. The church is always in danger of losing itself in that surrounding society that the New Testament calls "the world," human life organized and functioning without any thought of God. The process is subtle and slow. First, the church begins to admire the world. Next it tries to appeal to the world. Then it adopts the standards and methods of the world. In the end the church has nothing to bring to the world because they are so much alike. That is why everything that goes by the name cannot justly be called "the church."

Organization and Organism

What is the church? Is it an earthly institution often in danger of deadly compromise with secular culture? Or is it

144

a living spiritual organism nurtured by the life from God?

It is in a sense both organization and organism. Like Jesus, it is both earthly and heavenly. It is in the world without drawing its life from human sources. It is an organization in time and an organism in touch with eternity. It has a mission to men and a life from God. That is how the church exists: stretched in the tension between structure and spirit.

In one sense, the church is an institution, like other institutions of men. It has boundaries that set it apart from other agencies in society. It has a history that can be studied. It has ceremonies to observe at special times and designated places for its worship. In short, the church cannot escape history; it can only fulfill its mission as an organization.

Some Christians do not want to accept that fact. They try to release the church from time and space. They want to deliver the true people of God from the embarrassment of officials and property and customs.

But all such attempts prove unsuccessful in the end. To free Christianity from history and culture one must make it a philosophy of noble ideals. But the gospel has never been good advice; it is good news. God acted in time; and he still does. That is why the church is in one sense an institution. It lives and serves in time.

In another sense, the church is a spiritual organism, a living body in society. Although it consists of men and women, it is impelled by the purpose of God and sustained by the presence of God. This relation to God determines the nature and mission of the church. It is the community that God gathers; the worship that he inspires; the mission that he sends. That mission is to enlist a people loyal to Jesus Christ, to empower them by the new life of the Spirit, and send them back into the world to witness and to care in Jesus' name.

At the heart of the Bible's description of the church is the idea of call. It is cradled in the term most often used to designate the church. The Greek term *ekklesia* is built upon the root of the verb meaning "to call." The *ekklesia* is the assembly or community called together by God.[2]

The Call of God

The church, as the Bible describes it, is more than an aggregation—people who have chosen to come together. It is a congregation, a people called together by the Word of God, the gospel of Christ's love and forgiveness. God comes first, then the church. His call to salvation precedes the gathering of the people. As Paul puts it, we are called into "the fellowship of God's Son" (1 Cor. 1:9).

What, then, is this life to which the church is called? What is God's purpose for his people in the world?

The New Testament makes clear that the church is the primary consequence of the redemptive acts of God in Christ. God sent Jesus as the Savior of men and women. That is the meaning of his name: the Lord is Savior. And as we have seen, he accomplished his mission magnificently. By his death on the cross and his resurrection from the grave, he removed every barrier to the presence of God. He opened the gates to the Hidden World.

Confirmation of Jesus' success came with the miraculous descent of the Holy Spirit at Pentecost. The Spirit came not only to confirm the merit of the Sacrifice; he came just as importantly to create a new people of God. All that Jesus secured for the people of God, the Spirit came to deliver. "I am come," Jesus once said, "that they might have life" (John 10:10, KJV). He obtained it and the Holy Spirit delivered it. Those who receive it are the People of God, the church of the Living God.

Scriptures use a number of images to describe the nature and mission of the church. But three of the most common images highlight the church's special relationship with the Holy Trinity: Father, Son, and Holy Spirit.

Peter, for example, writes to "God's elect" throughout Asia Minor (today's Turkey), and he reminds them that they are "chosen according to the foreknowledge of God the Father, by the sanctifying work of the Spirit, for obedience to Jesus Christ and sprinkling by his blood" (1 Peter 1:2). The Father chooses the church, the Spirit sanctifies it, and the Son atones for it. This line of thought leads to three of the most widely used images of the church in Christian writings: the family of God, the body of Christ, and the temple of the Spirit.

The Family of God

The idea of the family of God is implicit in the prayer Jesus taught his disciples to pray. When you pray, he said, say, "our Father." The sense of family is there. We do not pray, "my Father"; we pray, "our Father."

This life in God's family suggests a special relationship to God. Within the church God is no longer some impersonal Power in the universe, some invisible, ill-defined Fear that clouds the future. No! He is the one Jesus taught us to call "heavenly Father."

The apostle Paul recognized the same relationship when he reminded the Ephesian Christians that they were no longer foreigners and aliens in God's eyes. They were "members of God's household" (Eph. 2:19).

The church addresses a deep-seated need in the human heart—the need to belong, to be a part of a significant community. The hosts of human organizations testify to this need: clubs, gangs, tribes, lodges, unions, fraternities—the list is almost endless.

Man, it seems, is made to belong. What, after all, is the most excruciating punishment in penal institutions? Solitary confinement. Why? Because loneliness is hell. God created human beings for loving fellowship, and the marred image of God in man witnesses to this thirst that cannot be quenched. The gospel is God's invitation to come to Christ and drink. Those who do come find that fellowship in the family of God.

This portrait of the church as God's family assumes unusual tones in the light of the idea of "the new covenant." The term *covenant* has almost dropped from our vocabulary, but in biblical times covenants were as common as contracts in our day. They were the acceptable way of establishing relationships. A covenant bound friend to friend (1 Sam. 18:3), or established water rights between two tribal leaders (Gen. 21:22–32), or expressed the terms of peace between two kings (1 Kings 20:34). It was a ready concept to express the relation between God and his people.

In both instances—the old covenant between the Lord and Israel and the new covenant between the Lord and the church—God prepared his people to accept the covenant by some dramatic act. He brought his people to the solemn assembly at Mount Sinai by miraculously delivering them from the hands of the Egyptians. There, after pointing to their exodus from Egypt, God said to Israel, "I bore you on eagles' wings and brought you to myself" (Ex. 19:4, RSV). The heart of the old covenant was this special relationship between the Lord and his people.

The new covenant between God and the church was established by the death and resurrection of Jesus. On the night of his betrayal, Jesus told his disciples that his death, depicted by the cup of his last supper with them, was "the new covenant in my blood." Unlike the old covenant expressed in laws written on stone, this covenant was etched by the Spirit on the hearts and consciences of Christian believers, just as the prophets had predicted it would be.

It is important to stress that this covenant with God was not a bargain that men struck with the Almighty. Pagan religions were filled with such ideas of covenants. Their devotees were desperately trying somehow to please the gods in order to enter into an agreement and escape their wrath.

In striking contrast, Israel's covenant was not one they offered to God. On the contrary, God took the initiative. By delivering Israel from Egyptian slavery he graciously presented the covenant to them. Similarly, in the cross and resurrection of Jesus, God offers himself to believers freely. His grace, his surprising love, and his forgiveness are extended to his people long before they turn and receive his mercy.

The recognition of this grace of God in the covenant inspires the church to sing with Samuel Davies,

> O may this strange, this matchless grace,
> This Godlike miracle of love,

Fill the whole earth with grateful praise,
And all th' angelic choirs above.
Who is a pardoning God like Thee?
Or who has grace so rich and free?
—*Great God of Wonders*

The Body of Christ

The second biblical image of the church is the body of Christ.
The meaning of the expression is not self-evident. In recent years
many Christians have mistakenly taken the phrase to mean "the
body of Christians," a collection of individual believers. The
church obviously includes people, but the Bible does not say
"the body of Christians." It says "the body of Christ." Christians
are members of the body; they represent the diversity. The body
is Christ's; he creates the unity.

Another possible understanding of the expression is "the community that belongs to Christ." This view takes "of Christ" as
a possessive and therefore sets the church off from other bodies.
Such a view, however, leaves Christ aside, much as an owner
of a horse is something totally different than the animal itself.

While it is true, in one sense, that the church belongs to
Christ—he "purchased" it with his blood—the idea the apostle
seems to have in mind when he uses "the body of Christ" is
the intimate union of Christ with his people and the life-giving
energy he provides for them.

Interestingly, the apostle Paul never calls the church "the torso
of Christ," with the head as something different and presumably
separable from the torso. No, the body is an inclusive term, desig-
nating the torso, with its members, and the head. We should
not think of the church then as something apart from Christ.
The church is the body of Christ only when he is present and
included.

Certainly Jesus is more than another founder of a religion.
By his death and resurrection he does more than establish the
church; he constitutes it. He gives it reality. Like the head of
any body he directs the actions of the church. And like digested

food, he energizes the body as its life-giving power. Through this body, Christ continues his work of salvation in the world.

The Temple of the Spirit

The third figure the apostles use to describe the church is the building, the temple of the Spirit. Both Peter and Paul adopt the image. Peter, for example, in his first letter to "God's elect" in Asia Minor, says, "You also, like living stones, are being built into a spiritual house to be a holy priesthood, offering spiritual sacrifices acceptable to God through Jesus Christ" (1 Peter 2:5).

The image is obviously mixed. The church is both the building, growing by the addition of each living stone (believer), and the priesthood that offers sacrifices of praise to God in the temple.

Peter's intention, however, is clear enough. The church, in his image, is the spiritual fulfillment of the whole temple experience maintained in Israel for centuries. God who once appeared in the holy place in Jerusalem now lives in the church by his Spirit. And the cornerstone of the building which determines the purpose of every other living stone is Jesus Christ. He is the determining One. Men and women either find God's purpose for them and are added to this spiritual temple under construction, or else they stumble in unbelief over the Cornerstone, Jesus Christ, and are crushed.

In Christianity, then, religion acceptable to God is not dependent upon holy rites conducted in sacred buildings. God's temple is the church. He comes to men who come to him through the great High Priest, and these are added to his temple by being aligned with the Cornerstone. God's chosen sanctuary is his people.

Within this spiritual temple all who are joined to Jesus Christ by faith share in the priesthood. In contrast to Judaism, in which only a single tribe functioned as priests, Christianity knows no special priesthood. All who come to God by faith in Christ share in the service of the sanctuary. What was unthinkable in Judaism is fundamental in Christianity. Proselytes become priests! The whole community of faith offers sacrifice.

The sacrifices are no longer animals slain in prescribed ceremonies. They are spiritual and moral. The sacrifices of the church are obedience to God, the praises of God, a contrite spirit, and practical service to needy people. This worship and service is pleasing to God because it is brought through Jesus Christ.

These images of the church reveal the significant ways that Christianity broke through the restrictive institutions of Judaism and emerged as a universal faith. A distinctive priesthood serving in a distinctive temple for a distinctive people with a distinctive tradition was now a thing of the past. The church had no special priesthood and no special building in a special place. The gospel is for all peoples in all places. Faith in Christ introduces a believer immediately into a universal confessional community which spans time and place.

Precisely because the church is for all people it can find embodiment everywhere. Believers are drawn by the Spirit to meet with those living in the same vicinity who profess this same faith-loyalty to Jesus Christ. This is why the New Testament writers speak of the church (*ekklesia*) in either of these senses. It is the universal body of all who profess faith in Jesus Christ as Savior and Lord. But at the same time, it is the local assembly of those in a given place who make that same profession.

The New Testament never suggests a conflict between the universal confessional community and the local gathered community. Apparently, the apostles thought of only one church because there is only one Savior and Lord of the church. In the Bible the church is not defined in terms of how many people make it up, but in terms of the distinctive life of God within the community.

Think of binoculars. As we look through the eyepieces, a bird is greatly magnified. But if you turn the binoculars around and look at a goldfinch through the lens end, it is greatly reduced. In all respects except size it is the same bird. It is the same principle with the church.

In the day-to-day life of the Christian it is important that the church have a tangible presence. It must appear in a particular place and at a particular time—for example, the First Presbyterian

Church of Springfield, Idaho, in 1985. Such a concrete expression of the church makes the community of faith a living reality. It is no mere abstraction. It is here and now, pointing to the presence of the people of God. But in the local church the people of God have faces.

Some Christians have tried to equate the universal church and the kingdom of God. That has often proved to be a foolhardy move. Such an equation tends to encourage the church to grasp for earthly power and to abuse it. The Bible indicates that the kingdom of God is God's rule and reign. The church is only the sphere where this has begun. P. T. Forsyth, the British theologian, once called the church "the kingdom in the making."

At the same time the church is the servant of the kingdom. By announcing the good news of Christ's appearing and the forgiveness available to men and women, it is inviting people to surrender to the reign of Christ. The Lordship, however, is always Christ's.

We also need to draw a clear distinction between the church and the state. In the Christian view of God's will in the world, the state is not simply a product of human design. It is a providential means of protecting society from the destructive forces of human nature and of fostering civility in public life. Some theologians call this the "strange work of Christ." Even among those who do not profess to follow him, Christ works invisibly to achieve civil order. As the apostle Paul put it: "The authorities that exist have been established by God" (Rom. 13:1).

In that sense, the church and the state complement each other. They both strive for human well-being. Their means, however, differ. The state relies on might and coercion. The church depends upon the vigorous announcement of the truth, and the visible demonstration of it in the world.

With these images and distinctions in mind we can now return to our original question. When Christians confess their faith "in the Holy Catholic Church," as they have done since the early third century, what do they have in mind? Some institution? What is the point of confessing faith in an institution? The point is Christians have always believed the church is more than an institution. It is the family of God, the body of Christ, and the temple of the Spirit.

Faith in the church in this sense acknowledges that we cannot live the Christian life in isolation, like a religious Robinson Crusoe. Membership in the church is not some optional extra. The fact is we cannot be fully Christian without belonging to the church. As we study the New Testament we find that to be a Christian is to be "in Christ." This means being a member of the new society of which Christ is the living Head—the church. The New Testament knows nothing of unattached Christians.

Consider the matter in a more mundane way. What would we think of a man who said that he wanted to be a soldier, but insisted that he could be a perfectly good one without joining the army? An unattached soldier is nonsense—so is the notion of a solitary Christian.

In short, membership in the church, far from being a matter of personal choice, is a spiritual necessity. All true Christian experience is ecclesiastical experience, experience gained, enriched, and matured in the presence of Christ and his people.

15

Basic Steps

Billy Sunday, the early twentieth-century American evangelist, once said, "Going to church don't make a man a Christian any more than going to a stable makes a man a horse."

Many people questioned Sunday's style but no one missed his point. It is possible to trust in a religious institution which cannot save in order to hide from the only God who can. But if the purpose of the church is not to make us Christians, what is it?

As we have seen, when Christians confess their belief in the church, as they have done down through the Christian centuries, they have in mind something more than another human institution. Belief in the church means faith in the life of God found in the church.

It is always possible to see the outward behavior of the church—its worship services or its impact on society—and to dismiss it as another "thing," a place to go, perhaps, or a program to operate. Such views are reflected in our conversation. We speak of "going to church" or "directing the program." Both suggest that the church is under human control.

But the church is not really a "thing." The moment you think of it as a "thing" you go astray. You cannot leave God out of the picture. The church is God's people. By his Spirit he lives within the community, shaping its life and character. That means the purpose of the church is to honor God's name and to serve his cause.

The church experiences the life of God in two fundamental ways: in the gathering and in the scattering of the people of God—in worship and in service. The first is for the growth of the body in the love of God; the second is for the work of the body for the needs of people. One is the inward journey of faith; the other is the outward journey of faith. Either way, in a secular society it is always possible for the church to miss the purpose of God.

The Gathered Church

The church is often tempted to turn its gathering into a distortion of God's purpose. It is easy to think of God's grace, his gift of transforming love, as a commodity and the church as a religious establishment for the distribution of goods and services to the community. God has stocked the shelves with religious merchandise such as worship, counseling, fellowship, and instruction. In this arrangement church leaders serve as the proprietors of the retail outlet. They direct the distribution of the spiritual services to the customers.

This institutional view of the church prides itself in the legality of the franchise, the quality of its goods, and the authority of its proprietors. It measures success in terms of satisfied customers, so the church becomes a business—God's business.

But the church can veer just as quickly from God's purpose as it scatters throughout a city. If the church is primarily a movement in society supporting all the right causes, it is easy to think of it as a civil demonstration, a group of people marching together for a common goal—the improvement of man's life on earth. Unlike the institution that emphasizes its authorization and its goods, the demonstration measures its success in terms of social benefits—fair housing, for example, or women's rights.

The demonstration image can also allow the secular world to intrude. It can subvert the purpose of God by making the

humanitarian impulse basic. The needs of men can undercut the
purposes of God.

The Ministry of the Word

The only corrective for these perversions is a clear vision of
the church under the Word of God. The community of faith
obedient to the Lord's purpose must maintain a balance between
gathering for the renewal of the life of God in the body and
scattering for the ministry of the Word of God in the world.
In both cases the Word of God is the essential element.

"The Word," said Martin Luther, "is the one perpetual and
infallible mark of the Church." When the church gathers it must
be the Word of God that it hears; when the church scatters it
must be the Word of God it shares.

The Word of God is a biblical expression; but its meaning is
not self evident. What do we mean by the Word of God? Basically
it means anything God does or says to communicate himself to
humanity. It is God actively making himself known to us.

The supreme way God has done this is in the incarnation—
Jesus Christ, God's living Word. God broke through the invisibil-
ity of the Hidden World and communicated himself to us by
sending his Son. Christians call him Immanuel, meaning "God
with us."

Scripture and Sacrament

How does God communicate the Word to people today? [1] He
does it in three ways:

First—through the Scriptures, the written Word of God. The
church describes these writings as the Word of God because in
them God makes himself known as Creator and Redeemer. They
tell the story of God's redeeming work in such a way that the
story in turn becomes an act of God upon the lives of those
who hear it and take its message personally.

Second—through the gospel, the spoken Word of God. The

Bible must be accepted as the truth and communicated by those who understand it. It must be set forth in living thought and speech. "Faith," said the apostle, "cometh by hearing, and hearing by the Word of God" (Rom. 10:17, KJV). So it is not the Bible as a dead book, but the message of the Bible understood, accepted, and proclaimed that is the medium of the Spirit of God in the church. It is the Spirit and the Word. The Spirit is the courier of God; the Word is his communique.

The church has used a host of means to communicate this message of God. In the gathered community, it has most often used music, Scripture reading, creeds, testimony, art, and mainly preaching to relate the Word of God to contemporary believers. Preaching links the first-century events recorded in the Bible to the life of men and women today. It applies the timeless truth of God to human tragedies and celebrations, to death and birth, to depression and elation. That is why the spoken Word of God is a constituting element in the continuing life of the church.

Third—through the sacraments, the Word of God enacted. Christians have always held that two ritual observances, instituted by Jesus Christ himself, are vital elements in the worship of the people of God. These are baptism and the Lord's Supper. Some Christians consider them important symbols of that grace of God received through faith in Jesus; other Christians assert that the two rituals actually confer the spiritual life which they picture. In both cases, Christians maintain that the ceremonies are for perpetual observance in the church. Most Christians call them sacraments. Others prefer the word "ordinances."

To the secular-minded person these two ceremonies probably appear silly: A gathering of otherwise sensible adults witnessing a friend being plunged beneath water, or a gathering around a table to eat bits of dried bread and take sips of diluted wine. What is this all about?

The term "sacrament" comes from a Latin word *sacramentum.* It was originally an oath of allegiance the Roman soldier took to his emperor. When the Christians took over the term they thought of those ceremonies that bound them in loyalty to Christ, the Captain of their salvation. The term "ordinance" stresses the same basic idea of Christ's authority. It reminds us that he ordained these two ceremonies for perpetual observance.

The sacraments, then, are visible signs of a spiritual reality, Christ's encounter with his people. In the sacraments the word of forgiveness and grace is depicted within the church. They are enacted sermons. They appeal to our souls through our senses and, by the witness of the Holy Spirit, they make the Savior real to his people.

Baptism

The first sacrament (or ordinance), baptism, is the rite by which a believer is inducted into the fellowship of the church. That has been the Christian practice ever since the days of the apostles.

The idea apparently came from Jesus. He accepted baptism at the hands of his cousin John the Baptist, whose preaching linked the outward ceremony with inward repentance. Jesus endorsed the same practice and urged his disciples to make other disciples and baptize them in the name of the Father, Son, and Holy Spirit. By this command he related baptism to the total saving work of the Trinity and prescribed it as the universal practice of the church.

The apostle Paul gave the early churches the most extensive theological explanation of baptism. He spelled out its significance in terms of death and resurrection. He told the Roman believers that retributive justice cannot be executed upon a dead man. So the Christian, united by faith to the death of Christ, is free from the condemnation of sin and through the resurrection of Christ he shares a totally new life. Baptism is the depiction of this spiritually transforming experience.

Over the centuries Christians have debated what baptism accomplishes, to whom it should be administered, and how much water should be used. The New Testament itself seems to emphasize the central importance of faith for baptism. It is administered to those who stand humbly before God in the grace and mercy of God revealed in the death and resurrection of Jesus.

At the moment of baptism the Christian makes an irrevocable commitment to Christ, whose death provides him forgiveness and whose life from the dead makes possible his power to live by faith. By this confession of faith in baptism he enters a new relationship with God and is added to the fellowship of the Spirit in the life of the church.

By accepting baptism, the Christian devotes himself to spiritual growth and to the standards of the fellowship into which he has been inducted. So baptism is more than a religious ceremony; it is a moral and spiritual pledge of devotion to Christ and to his people.

The Lord's Supper

The second sacrament is the memorial meal instituted by Jesus on the eve of his death on the cross. As he celebrated the Jewish Passover with his disciples, he gave them bread to eat and wine to drink and said, "This is my body, broken for you . . . . This is my blood of the new covenant, which is shed for many." Since that hour the ceremony has served as the focal point of Christian worship.

Christians have differing names for the sacred meal. Some, recalling its institution by Christ, call it the Lord's Supper. Others call it Holy Communion, as a reminder of the fellowship of believers with their Lord and with other believers. Some call it the Eucharist, which means thanksgiving. These want to stress that the people of God receive the bread and the cup with grateful joy. Under whatever name, however, Christians see the reminder of the gospel and that forgiveness of sin available to the believer.

The primary significance of the Lord's Supper is the representation of Christ's death as the basis of the new covenant between God and his people. The breaking of Christ's body and the shedding of his blood made the sacrifice necessary to reconcile men to God. In the sacred meal bread and wine enter the body and are assimilated into the physical body to contribute to its life and health—a dramatic picture of the life of Christ entering spiritually into the life of the grateful believer. Thus, the Lord's Supper constantly renews the saving power of Christ for the believing community and each member of it.

By instituting this meal for perpetual observance, Jesus apparently intended to keep alive the memory of his purpose for his disciples. They were to serve him until he returned to them. He gave few details of their mission, but he clearly envisioned a program of extending the message of his sacrifice and the invitation to submit to his reign in peoples' hearts. Knowing of his own departure, he gave to his disciples the stimulus to hope for his return and reason to pursue his purposes until he did.

By these two sacraments, then, the Lord provided for the initiation and the nurture of the believer in the family of God. By baptism the believer declares his faith in Jesus Christ's gift of forgiveness of sin; and by his public expression of dependence upon the life of Christ he maintains his unity with Christ and his people.

The Mission of the Church

The Bible indicates that the church that gathers must also be the church that scatters. The two callings are inextricably united: worship and mission. They create a spiritual rhythm for the Christian life. There is no proclamation to the world without a community distinct from the rest of society to do the proclaiming. And at the same time the call to come to Christ is an invitation to men and women to enter into a new community, distinct from the world. They can only learn of Christ with Christ's people, the church.

In recent years people inside the church as well as those outside have come to think of the church as an instrument of human progress or of social revolution. Somewhere men and women got the notion that the church is supposed to be a way to achieve something worthwhile in the secular world, something that secularism can measure and approve. In other words, the church is a means to a higher end.

Few people, however, think of the church as an indispensable means to life's highest reality. They believe that it is something like catching a plane for Chicago. That is one way to go. But you might drive a car or board a train. You could even walk. The plane will get you there but it is not absolutely essential.

Christians, however, believe that the church is more like an orchestra for a symphony. The symphony can exist in the composer's mind and on paper, but it remains an abstraction until the one thing necessary is found to make it real for men and women, namely an orchestra. The composer may have a lawn mower or a dish washer. Both are excellent instruments for other purposes, but neither was designed to perform a symphony. Only an orchestra will meet that need.

In the same way only the church serves to carry the good news of salvation through Jesus Christ. Men and women may join the church or remain outside, but they are not at liberty to change the church into something it was not designed to be. Like an orchestra it fulfills its purpose only by being what it is.

And what is the church in the world? It is the body of Christ. It is God's answer to human need. It is light in the midst of darkness.

The Bible links the mission of the church to the mission of God. The God of the Bible goes forth seeking straying men and women. He called Abraham to leave his kindred and promised not only to bless him but to bless other nations through him (Gen. 12:1–3). He sent Moses to the oppressed Israelites in Egypt and delivered them from slavery. He sent a succession of prophets with promises and warnings for his people. Then at last, "in the fullness of time," he sent forth his Son.

This mission of the Son was the mission of all missions. During his public ministry he said he had come to seek and to save the lost. He sent forth his disciples preaching, teaching, and healing. Then when his enemies succeeded in nailing him to a cross, he sent his Spirit to empower his disciples to fulfill his final command: "Go into all the world and preach the gospel" (Mark 16:15, RSV). Jesus' mission was to be a model for his disciples. "As the Father has sent me," he said, "I am sending you" (John 20:21). The mission of the church arises from the mission of Jesus.

There is, however, a significant difference. By his death and resurrection Jesus Christ secured the salvation of men and women; by the power of his life-giving Spirit the church announces the salvation that Jesus secured.

We call this witness of the church "evangelism." That term is often misunderstood. It comes from a Greek word that means to announce the *evangelion,* the good news. In Christianity that can only mean the good news about Jesus' death and resurrection and his gift of the Spirit.

This is how worship and witness are linked. In worship we praise God for his salvation; in evangelism we tell others about this same salvation.

Elton Trueblood, the Quaker scholar, once compared evangelism to fire. Evangelism occurs, he said, when Christians are so ignited by their contact with Christ that they in turn set other fires. It is easy to determine when something is aflame. It ignites other material. Any fire that does not spread will eventually go out. A church without evangelism is a contradiction in terms, just as a fire that does not burn is a contradiction.[2]

In the end, then, Billy Sunday's down-to-earth wisdom is only a half-truth. The church as a religious institution cannot guarantee the life of God to a worshiper. But as the community of faith that God intended, the church can make available the Word of God and the grace of God for followers of Christ everywhere.

16

Forgiven Sinners

New York City has the Statue of Liberty, symbol of the ideal of the French Revolution, freedom from the oppression of unjust regimes, both civil and ecclesiastical. Rio de Janeiro has the statue of Christ the Redeemer, symbol of the message of Christianity, deliverance from enslavement to sin, death, and fear.

The Statue of Liberty rises in massive splendor out of New York Harbor and extends her light of freedom to all who come to the American shores. Christ the Redeemer stands atop 2300-foot Mount Corcovado. He is depicted not on the cross, as one might expect in a largely Roman Catholic country, but with outstretched arms, inviting the whole bustling city below to look to Jesus Christ for salvation.

When Christians say, "Look to Christ," what do they mean? What is salvation? And how do we receive it?

The Meaning of Salvation

Salvation is one of the basic ideas of Scripture, from the sacrifices of Abraham in Genesis to the songs of the redeemed in Revelation. In the Old Testament, salvation is closely linked with redemption. It means deliverance from some sort of confinement, such as slavery. In Israel's history this release is nearly always from some physical or political tight spot.

163

The best example is the deliverance from the bondage in Egypt, the Exodus. After Moses stretched out his hand over the threatening waters and led the children of Israel "through the sea on dry ground," they saw the Egyptian forces—chariots and horses—swept into the sea. And they knew they were free. "That day the Lord saved Israel from the hands of the Egyptians" (Exod. 14:30). Once delivered, Moses and the Israelites sang: "The Lord is my strength and my song; he has become my salvation" (Exod. 15:2).

This miraculous deliverance became the foundation of Israel's hope through scores of other dangers during the age of the judges, the kingdom of David and Solomon, and the titanic struggles with Assyria and Babylon. These experiences taught Israel to sing:

> No king is saved by the size of his army;
> No warrior escapes by his great strength.
> A horse is a vain hope for deliverance;
> despite all its great strength it cannot save.
> But the eyes of the Lord are on those who
> fear him,
> on those whose hope is in his unfailing love.
> (Ps. 33:16–18)

Israel came to see that liberation is never the work of man; God alone saves.

The New Testament, like the Old, does not define salvation. It chooses instead to proclaim it as an accomplished fact. In the New Testament, however, salvation is no longer a physical and provisional deliverance, such as an escape from some military threat. It is total liberation, ultimate deliverance (Rom. 1:16).

This deliverance, granted by God, is never described in terms of some gradual ascent to a higher level of existence. It is always pictured as a sharp break with the past, such as life from the grave. A saved person moves dramatically from enslavement to liberty, from death to life. That is salvation.

But what is a person saved from? He is saved from his sins (Matt. 1:21), from condemnation (John 3:17), from death

(Luke 6:9), and from the wrath of God (Rom. 5:9). Throughout its pages the New Testament stresses that no threat is as serious for man as the disapproval of God. Understandably, then, salvation consists fundamentally of the recovery of peace with God. It is the deliverance from the condemnation of God and entrance into the favor of God. When we think of the gift of salvation in personal terms, we can distinguish three fundamental aspects: initial salvation, continued salvation, and completed salvation.

Initial salvation embraces all that God does in a believer's life to initiate the life of God in the soul and establish a special, new relation with God. Continued salvation is a way of describing the believer's spiritual life, how he grows and matures in his relationship with God. Completed salvation deals with the finished product, what God intends for a believer in his perfected state.

In this chapter we want to concentrate on initial salvation, how the deliverance from fear and impotence and sin and death begins. In the next chapter we will examine how it continues and, in chapter 20, how it is completed.

Estranged from God, man faces two basic spiritual needs. First, he needs to be restored to God's fellowship. He is guilty before God and somehow he must find forgiveness. Second, he needs power to change. His sin reveals his spiritual impotence. If his life is to be different, someone will have to show him how to overcome his failures and find the strength to be a new person. In short, he needs something done *for* him and something done *in* him.

Justification by Faith

One way to describe initial salvation is by a term often used by the apostle Paul. It is justification. Paul asks whether a person can be justified before God by strictly observing the Jewish law. Or, to put it another way, can a sinner be regarded as righteous by God on the basis of his obedience to God's commands?

The term "justify" comes from the courtroom. It refers to a legal verdict. It means "acquit." It is not concerned with a person's righteous character, but is concerned with his relationship to God and his just law. Is a person who has sinned in the past acquitted by God if he has kept the law's commands? Paul answers, "No." No man can keep the law in every point. That is impossible.

How, then, can a person be justified? Is there some way other than keeping the commands of God? Yes, says the apostle. In the Jewish law itself there is a provision for the offender to offer sacrifice to God for his sin. In this way sin can be cancelled and the spiritual rebel forgiven. Drawing upon the language of the sacrificial system, Paul asserts that the death of Jesus was a sacrifice for sin. He described it as an "expiation" or a "propitiation" (Rom. 3:25).

For generations Christian scholars have debated the meaning of these two terms. "Expiate" is a verb which has as its object not a person but a thing. The purpose of sacrifice, then, is to expiate sin. The offering of a sacrificial victim wipes out sin; it cancels sin so that it no longer stands between the offender and God.

"Propitiate," however, has as its object a person. It means to appease an offended person so that he is willing to forgive. In pagan religious language the word described ways to placate the angry gods who often broke out in fury against men. Such imagery compelled some scholars to reject the term for Christian theology lest the sacrifice of Christ suggest that God is some capricious pagan deity. They preferred "expiate."

The term "expiate," however, has significant weaknesses. It makes sin a thing that can be removed or erased. The heart of sin, as the Bible presents it, is the broken relationship between men and God. This alienation must be overcome. It requires some act that restores fellowship between God and rebels. It is not a question of the removal of some "thing" but of enmity and guilt.

"Propitiate" has the advantage of highlighting the personal effects of sin and the necessity of turning aside the wrath of God. The beauty of the gospel, according to Paul, is precisely in this fact: God himself offered Jesus as a propitiation for spiritual rebels. Justice and mercy met at the cross of Jesus.

Through the course of Christian history no one has seen this doctrine of justification more clearly than Martin Luther. The son of a Saxon miner, Luther had hopes of becoming a lawyer, until one day in 1505 he was caught in a severe thunderstorm. A bolt of lightning slapped him to the ground. Terrified, Luther called out to Catholicism's patroness of miners, "St. Anne, save me! And I'll become a monk."

Luther kept that vow. Obsessed with guilt, he entered the Augustinian monastery at Erfurt and proved to be a zealous monk. He pushed his body mercilessly, sometimes fasting for three days, sometimes sleeping without a blanket in freezing weather. Nothing seemed to relieve his tormented soul. No amount of penance, no soothing advice from his superiors could still Luther's conviction that in the sight of God he was a miserable, doomed sinner.

Relief eventually came through the Scriptures. Assigned to the chair of biblical studies at the University of Wittenberg, Luther became fascinated with the words of Christ from the cross, "My God, my God, why have you forsaken me?" Christ forsaken! How could our Lord be forsaken? Luther felt himself forsaken but he was a sinner. Christ was not. The answer had to lie in Christ's identity with sinful humanity. Was he forsaken in order to bear the punishment required by human sin?

Such questions opened before Luther a bold, new picture of God. Finally, in 1515, while pondering the apostle Paul's letter to the Romans, Luther came upon the words: "For therein is the righteousness of God revealed from faith to faith: as it is written, The just shall live by faith" (Rom. 1:17, KJV).

Here, at last, was Luther's answer to spiritual uncertainty. "Night and day I pondered," Luther later recalled, "until I saw the connection between the justice of God and the statement that 'the just shall live by faith.' Then I grasped that the justice of God is that righteousness by which through grace and sheer mercy God justifies us through faith. Thereupon I felt myself to be reborn and to have gone through open doors into paradise."

New Life in Christ

Luther's reference to a rebirth is appropriate. Another way of viewing initial salvation is captured in the term "regeneration." It means new life—a new birth. The apostle pointed to this reality when he wrote: God . . . made us alive with Christ "even when we were dead . . ." (Eph. 2:4–5). When Christians are saved they are "born again" into a new realm of existence.

In regeneration, a person's existence is fundamentally changed. He is made alive to the life of God. What was once repugnant to him is now a source of pleasure. A new sense of values, a new lifestyle, a new understanding of himself, a new creative energy are all evidences of the Spirit within him. He is a new person.

This new outlook echoes in one of our familiar hymns:

> May the mind of Christ my Savior
> Live in me from day to day,
> By His love and power controlling
> All I do and say.
>
> May the Word of God dwell richly
> In my heart from hour to hour,
> So that all may see I triumph
> Only through His power.
> —Kate B. Wilkinson
> *May the Mind of Christ, My Savior* [1]

This rebirth is no gradual process. It is a spontaneous, creative act of God. There is usually some preparation for it and some development of it, but the birth itself is spontaneous. A person is either alive to God or he is not. He is either a Christian or he is not.

"It may be hard," C. S. Lewis once said, "for an egg to turn into a bird; it would be a jolly sight harder for it to learn to fly while remaining an egg. We are like eggs at present. And you cannot go on indefinitely being an ordinary decent egg. We must be hatched or go bad." [2]

There is, of course, a difference between regeneration itself and the awareness of it. The first is an act of God in the soul. The second is the conscious response of man. Not everyone is immediately aware of the act of God. That is the reason one Christian should never insist that his experience be the standard for all others within the Christian community. Not everyone is immediately conscious of the influence of the Spirit in regeneration. The issue is not the way a person is regenerated but the fact of a person's regeneration.

Shortly before he was assassinated in 1968, Martin Luther King, Jr., speaking in Los Angeles, chose to close an address by quoting an old slave preacher who said,

> We ain't what we ought to be,
> and we ain't what we want to be,
> and we ain't what we're going to be
> but, thank God, we ain't what we was.

That is true, too, of the genuine Christian.

This initial salvation which restores a believer to God's fellowship can be considered from God's side and from man's side. There is an attitude that God reveals and a special response required of man.

Amazing Grace

God's attitude and work in man's salvation is captured in one word—grace. While it is clear throughout the Bible that men must accept God's offer of salvation, this decision is never a basis of boasting. Human achievement and pride are forever eliminated from salvation by God's grace, his surprising love for the undeserving.

The story of the saving work of God, which binds the various books of the Bible into a unified whole, is an account of the grace of God. Without grace there would never have been a chosen people, nor a story of salvation to tell.

The Old Testament term for grace (*chesed*), often translated "steadfast love," stands for God's continuing faithfulness to his covenant people. The psalmist taught Israel to sing:

> O give thanks to the Lord, for he is good,
>   for his steadfast love endures forever.
> O give thanks to the God of gods,
>   for his steadfast love endures forever.
> O give thanks to the Lord of lords,
>   for his steadfast love endures forever.
>   (Ps. 136:1–3, RSV)

It was God's grace that called Israel out of Egypt and it was grace that would not let her go (Exod. 15:13). The grace of God, then, is not a thing. It is God's attitude toward men. It is a personal relationship which God establishes and maintains.

The New Testament term (*charis*) underscores God's redemptive love which is always active in rescuing rebels and restoring them to his wealth and favor. The apostle Paul, as perhaps no other man, probed the depths and wonder of God's love. He saw Israel's rejection of Jesus Christ as the climax of a long history of unbelief and apostasy. But "the stone the builders rejected has become the capstone" (Ps. 118:22). Jesus Christ, once rejected and crucified, is the basis of a new covenant open to all people. Anyone can now be justified freely by God's grace through the redemption that is in Christ Jesus (Rom. 3:21–24). Forgiving love is the fountain of every other gift of grace flowing from the favor of God.

The human response to this initial salvation—including justification and regeneration—is captured in the term conversion. The word appears in many contexts today. Christians have no monopoly on it. Men and women can be converted from democratic convictions to communism, or from conservative economic views to liberal ones.

In the Christian faith the term takes special significance only in the new direction of a person's change. A believer shifts from loyalties that are essentially selfish to loyalties that are directed toward Christ. A Christian is converted from a self-driven life to a Christ-controlled life. That is the important point.

Repentance and Faith

In Christianity, conversion always has two basic elements—one is negative, the other is positive. The negative note appears in the term repentance; the positive note sounds in faith.

The Christian concept of repentance springs from two biblical terms. In the Old Testament, the Hebrew word suggests some "turning." In the New Testament, the Greek word indicates some "change of mind." So the Christian idea of repentance carries both ideas. It is a turning from the old way of life, dominated by selfish and sinful passions. It is also a change of mind—a new attitude—about God and Christ, and the direction of one's own life.

Repentance should never be confused with penance. That was an unfortunate error committed by Christians throughout the Middle Ages. They took Jesus' call to repentance in preparation for the kingdom (Matt. 4:17) as an obligation to perform acts of self-denial in order to gain grace and find forgiveness. True repentance, however, is more inward than it is outward. It begins with the repudiation of one's own spiritual worth and only then moves to any expression of self-denial.

Genuine repentance is also always linked with faith. They are flip sides of the same coin. As repentance is an inward turning from the old life, faith is the inward direction of the soul toward God, the Source of the new life. This faith is more than assent to the truths of the gospel. As we have seen, personal Christian faith moves beyond assent to personal trust in Jesus Christ as Savior. It is the essence of the relationship between the believer and God.

John Paton, the pioneer missionary to the New Hebrides Islands, was once translating the New Testament into the language of the islanders. He could find no word, however, to translate "faith." One day, after long hours of work, he slumped in his chair exhausted. "I'm so tired," said Paton, "I feel like resting all my weight on this chair." Instantly, he sat straight up and yelled, "Praise God, I've got my word." That is it. Faith means putting all your weight upon God. It is complete trust and commitment.[3]

Christians contend that "looking to Christ" in that sense brings salvation, a liberty that the Lady in New York Harbor has never known.

17

The Family Likeness

"Once, as I rode out into the woods for my health, in 1737," Jonathan Edwards wrote in his *Personal Narrative*, "having alighted from my horse in a retired place, to walk for divine contemplation and prayer, I had a view of the glory of the Son of God. The person of Christ appeared ineffably excellent. I felt an ardency of soul to be emptied and annihilated; to lie in the dust, and to be full of Christ alone; to trust in him; to live upon him; to serve and follow him." [1]

Unfortunately, about all that many Americans recall about Jonathan Edwards, the colonial genius, is his sermon "Sinners in the Hands of an Angry God." That has erroneously established his reputation as a hellfire-and-brimstone Puritan revivalist. That is tragic, because the man was not only one of America's great minds, he was also—as this quotation reveals—a great soul.

Edwards reminds us that the Christian life is more than doctrines to confess; it is also a Person to follow. But how does faith tap this knowledge of God? What does the Christian life look like?

Sinners and Saints

As we have seen, ordinary people suffer from two fundamental afflictions. They are estranged from God and they are spiritually sick. Therefore they need to be reconciled to God and they need to be made whole.

The salvation of God, as we initially experience it, is God's remedy for humanity's estrangement from God. It provides a way of reconciliation through the death and resurrection of Jesus Christ. Men and women may be justified in God's sight and receive the new life of the Spirit. But they must surrender all attempts at self-justification and trust in God's forgiveness. That is the beginning of salvation's story.

The Bible indicates that the transforming work of God only begins when a person experiences the birth of faith. As with any infant, that faith must be protected and nurtured and exercised. That is what the Christian life is all about.

In one sense the Christian believer is saved instantaneously. He is delivered from the deadly consequences of life without God. But in another sense he is not yet saved. He is not yet the person God had in mind when he was intercepted in his mad scramble toward ruin. He is not completely freed from the sin that persists in his thoughts and values and actions. So we say, "He is being saved."

That is why the apostle Paul speaks at times of "those who are being saved," just as he does of "those who are perishing." Believers have not yet reached heaven any more than unbelievers have reached hell (1 Cor. 1:18). The word for this process of salvation is "sanctification."

Unfortunately, the term creates problems because it sounds so religious. It is related to the term "holiness" because in the Bible "to sanctify" means "to make holy." So a "saint" is a "holy one." But who wants to be a saint? Holy people intimidate us. When we hear "holy" we usually think of "holier-than-thou" and we often confuse "sanctified" with "sanctimonious." As a result, we tend to associate the biblical expressions with some artificial and sometimes hypocritical religious person. And none of us wants to be that!

If we want to understand the Christian life we will have to work our way through this problem. The best place to begin is with some old ideas. In the Bible the basic meaning of the word *holy* is "separate" or "different." In Old Testament times something holy was set apart or reserved for God's use. Sacrificial animals, for example, were holy. In the same way certain days were *sanctified,* which means they were set apart for the worship of God.

So when the New Testament calls Christians "saints," it simply means that they are intended for God's special use. Whether singing his praise in the sanctuary or resisting injustices in the world, Christians are "the people of God."

It might help to think of the way Jesus was different. He did not put on pious airs. When he came into town, the common people welcomed him. They found him attractive and winsome. How was he different? Certainly not in his religiosity. He had character, integrity, and purpose. He was not enslaved to peer pressure or public opinion. As he helped people in agonizing need, he was remarkably free of self-interest. When tempted to think of Number One, he resisted the temptation and submitted to something higher in life. He had come, he said, to do the Father's will.

A close look at Christ is important because the first way the New Testament describes holiness is in terms of "Christlikeness." Paul tells the Corinthians, "We . . . are being transformed into his likeness with ever-increasing glory, which comes from the Lord, who is the Spirit" (2 Cor. 3:18). Peter stresses the same idea in his first letter. He urges his readers: "Just as he who called you is holy, so be holy in all you do; for it is written: 'Be holy, because I am holy'" (1 Peter 1:15–16). Sanctification, then, is day-by-day growth in Christlikeness.

The Law of Likeness

Life itself seems to reveal a law of likeness. A person becomes what he admires. In nature, for example, the sunflower turns its face to the rising sun and grows by weaving the sunbeams into the fabric of its existence. The parallel in Christian experience is holiness. When men and women make Jesus Christ the center of their loyalty and love they grow in Christlikeness.

American literature holds a memorable illustration of this law. It comes from Nathaniel Hawthorne's story of "The Great Stone Face." A boy named Ernest grew up in a beautiful valley hidden among the mountains. The valley was marked by an interesting feature of nature. On a high mountain crag overlooking the valley, the rocks took the form of a human face, a strong, noble face that inspired wonder in anyone who looked at it intently.

In the valley was a legend that someday a great and noble person would return to the community who would resemble the face on the mountain. He would be a native son who had grown up there, had gone out and achieved fame in the world outside, and then had returned to bring wonderful benefits to people in the valley.

Ernest's mother explained this legend to her little son, and he grew up looking often toward the mountain face, longing for the great one to come. By and by when he was a young man the news spread that the legend was about to be fulfilled. A son of the valley had gone out and made a fortune and was now returning to spend his last years with his old neighbors. Rumors swept through the valley that he looked exactly like the face on the mountain. In due time he arrived and the crowd cheered, believing the prophecy had come true. When Ernest saw him, however, he was disappointed. The man's calculating profile had none of the nobility that characterized the Great Stone Face.

Time passed and Ernest grew older. His neighbors sought him out for counsel and comfort. Inspired by the face on the mountain, he proved to be a friend of all. Every few years a new rumor arose; another aspirant would come back to the valley, the supposed fulfillment of the legend. The second to arrive was a famous general from the wars, "Old Blood-and-Thunder." The third was a statesman aspiring to his country's highest office, "Old Stony Phiz." Each time, filled with wishful thinking, the excited crowd was sure that the long awaited benefactor had arrived; but each time, as Ernest looked to verify the report, he was disappointed.

Finally, there returned to the valley a poet whose exalted verse Ernest had come to admire. Maybe he was the fulfillment of the great hope. But when Ernest suggested the idea, the poet quickly denied it. He explained that while his words reflected the noble image, his life had not always done so. One evening, however, as the poet sat with the other neighbors and listened to Ernest offer encouragement and help to his friends, the sunset glow upon the prophetic face on the mountain shone also on Ernest's face and the poet cried out, "Look! Look! Ernest is the likeness of the Great Stone Face!" Then all the people looked and saw that what the deep-sighted poet had said was true.

That is one way of describing the Christian life. It is growing in Christlikeness.

A second way of looking at sanctification, the Christian's progress in faith, is through a new realm of existence. The believer, we read, is in Christ. What does that mean? We might compare the image to weightlessness. When the space programs of the United States and the Soviet Union were launched, space travelers encountered an unusual reality, life in weightlessness. It was a whole new realm of existence and called for special equipment to guarantee human survival in a world without gravity. Scenes of life in the realm of weightlessness soon became common to television viewers, with pictures of food or tools or even human beings drifting about a space ship aimlessly.

Life in Christ

The new realm in which the believer finds himself is in Christ. The apostle Paul uses the expression in his letters no less than 160 times. It is obviously fundamental to his view of the Christian life. "If anyone is in Christ," he writes, "he is a new creation; the old has gone, the new has come!" (2 Cor. 5:17). The believer's spiritual life begins "in Christ" and continues "in him." Paul urges the Colossians: "Just as you received Christ Jesus as Lord, continue to live in him, rooted and built up in him" (Col. 2:6).

What the apostle intended by this expression is not entirely clear. Adolf Deissmann was the German scholar who first drew attention to the importance of the phrase in the theology of Paul. He held that the expression indicates a spiritual atmosphere in which the believer lives—something like a bird living in the air, or as we have suggested, astronauts in weightlessness.[2]

Other scholars questioned an interpretation that suggests making Christ an atmosphere rather than a person. They prefer to think of Christ's authority or his power to command obedience. To be in Christ is to be in submission to his will.

The truth of the matter probably lies in the combination of the two views. A Christian is in Christ in the sense that he is united to him by faith and is brought increasingly into the sphere of his sovereign authority. In this new spiritual environment the Christian finds spiritual life and maturity.

Free at Last

A third way to think of the Christian life is freedom from the slavery of self-centeredness. Once in conversation with some proud Jews, Jesus said, "If you hold to my teaching, you are really my disciples. Then you will know the truth, and the truth will set you free."

"We are Abraham's descendants," they replied, "and have never been slaves of anyone."

"I tell you the truth," said Jesus, "everyone who sins is a slave to sin . . . . So if the Son sets you free, you will be free indeed" (John 8:31–36).

Anyone who has ever tried to stop smoking, lose weight, or control his passions in any way will know what Jesus meant. Our appetites, our ego, our greed—these are like thick-walled prisons to anyone who has tried to find deliverance.

This is not the contemporary view of personal freedom. I know. Most moderns think that freedom is life without responsibility or commitments, a rootless lifestyle free to follow the least whim or impulse. Surely that is a route to happiness. Some fledgling poet caught the mood in a bit of verse:

> I'm tickled to death I'm single.
> I'm tickled to death I'm free.
> I've got my independence.
> I've got the front door key.[3]

As long as we think of freedom in terms of freedom from restraints, we will never understand Jesus. He never accepted this contemporary gospel. He held a more realistic view of human nature. He knew that the person who is completely free to do as he pleases is soon a slave to his own passions.

Jesus points instead to freedom for a purpose. We can see the importance of purpose all around us. Driving through many small towns you will often find Main Street bisected by a set of railroad tracks. You will hear a bell ringing and find red lights flashing as a gate drops across the highway. Within a few seconds a powerful passenger train roars by, thundering west on two narrow rails. What is freedom for that train?

Or change the scene. When our children were youngsters we had a tropical fish aquarium. With a shaft of light above and air bubbles supplying oxygen, the fish could swim gracefully around the aquarium and give the children a lot of enjoyment. Once in awhile, however, we would come home and find a swordtail or an angelfish out on the floor near the aquarium—dead as a mounted moose. What was freedom for that fish?

Freedom, you see, is the condition that allows us to fulfill the purpose for which we were designed. As long as we insist on making life a full-time ego trip we will never know freedom. As the train was made for the rails, as fish were made for water, we were made for God. That is why Augustine, the early church bishop, once said, "Slavery to God is perfect freedom. "And that is why Charles Wesley wrote:

> My chains fell off,
> My heart was free;
> I rose, went forth
> and followed Thee.
> —*And Can It Be*
> *That I Should Gain?*

Trust and Obey

Is this transformation in Christ's likeness, this mounting strength "in Christ," this increasing freedom to follow Christ, the work of God, or is it the responsibility of believers? We have often heard, "God helps those who help themselves." We have heard it so often we may think it comes from the Bible. It doesn't. It has an element of truth no doubt, but it can also mislead us. We may be tempted to think of God as the great booster who helps us over the humps in life—something like the extra horsepower we need when life is all uphill.

But anyone familiar with the Bible will recognize that God is more than that, much more. He is not in the business of rubber-stamping our proposals and plans. He is the beginning as well as the end. He never surrenders the initiative to anyone. He is the first and the last. He is Lord.

Does that mean, then, that I am supposed to sit back and take it easy? Am I supposed to relax and wait for the skies to open? That doesn't sound like the apostolic letters. What about fighting the good fight, running the race and finishing the course?

The issue of "How much does God do and how much do I do?" is fundamental to the Christian life. It is not an abstract question. It touches almost every area of Christian experience. Take public worship as an example. Am I obligated to be at the sanctuary every time the door is open? How will the church survive if I do not support its services?

Put in this way that sounds like an awesome burden for a Christian to carry. But would we want to flip the coin and argue the other side? God doesn't need our help. It really doesn't matter whether Christians support the church or not. God has hidden resources, and human failure will never frustrate his plans.

What is the solution to this problem? We find a possible answer in Colossians 1:24–29. Paul is speaking there about his preaching of the gospel. He says, "To this end I labor, struggling with all the energy which so powerfully works in me." He could have made the same point about prayer, or giving, or reading the Scriptures, or any other Christian activity, because the same truth applies. Paul preaches zealously because of the nature of the gospel, a mystery "now disclosed to the saints." It is nothing less than "Christ in you, the hope of glory."

The gospel announces that Christ has not only come to pay

the awful price for sin on the cross. He has also come to live within his people. Believers are no longer confronted with commands from an outside master; they are children of God, imbued with the life of their Father. They have actually received his life and power. This is the gospel and it is the resolution of the problem of our initiative or God's.

What specifically does the Christian do to enlarge the life of God in the soul? Christians have always taken one of two positions on that question.

Some Christians tend to look to the ministry of the church for their growth in grace. We might call them institutional believers. They have been taught to believe that the grace of God is associated with the sacraments of the church. By faithfully attending church and receiving the teaching and counsel and sacraments of the institution that Jesus established, they hope to grow in their knowledge and likeness of him.

Other Christians take a more personal approach to growth in grace. They are less dependent upon the church and more inclined to practice personal spiritual disciplines. We might call these Christians individual believers. They tend to rely less on the church and more on the Bible for their knowledge of God and their concept of Christian conduct. They do not resist Christian gatherings but they tend to see corporate Christianity as a means to the end of personal holiness.

The truth of the matter probably blends both of these emphases. The church strengthens our Christian faith by reminding us that God's purpose is a people who embody his truth and grace. The church lifts faith out of the inner world of the soul and plants it in a generation-spanning tradition sustained by the gospel. It insists that true faith arises from the great redemptive acts of God in history.

At the same time, the Bible reminds us time and time again that institutions without the renewing power of the Spirit within the soul are barriers to true faith. Many times in the past, faith in the gospel has had to resist Christian officials and traditions and ceremonies. Only an intensely personal relationship with God is capable of igniting the flames of spiritual renewal.

Christians of both commitments, however, have agreed that two practices are absolutely indispensable for Christian holiness. They are prayer and the reception of the Word of God.

Prayer is the conversation of the soul with God. It is the result of the new life brought by the regenerating Spirit. The apostle Paul expressed it this way: "You received the Spirit of sonship. And by him we cry 'Abba, Father' " (Rom. 8:15). Prayer, then, is a sign of the family likeness, the inward affinity of the soul for God.

Prayer takes many forms: praise, petition, intercession, thanksgiving, adoration. But whatever the expression, it is the means given by God to commune with him. So Christians pray both corporately in public worship and personally in quiet communion.

The complement to prayer is the Word of God. Through the retelling of Scripture's story we discover what God is like and what he expects of us. And that for the Christian is food and drink. "Faith comes from hearing the message," wrote the apostle, "and the message is heard through the Word of Christ" (Rom. 10:17).

The one word for the Christian life is Christ. That is why Jonathan Edwards's lonely figure in the New England woods is a fit symbol for us all. Alone before God, he found that his deepest longing was to trust in Christ, to live upon him, to serve and follow him.

18

The Difference Faith Makes

In Plato's *Republic,* Socrates outlines his vision of the ideal commonwealth. When someone asks him where a person might find such a society, the wise man has to admit that no state on earth conforms to his ideal.

"But in heaven," he says, "perhaps there is a pattern of it laid up for the one who wants to behold, and beholding to found such a city in his own soul. It makes no difference whether it exists anywhere or ever will exist. For he would live in the ways of that city only and of no other."

Like Socrates, Christians believe that the kingdom of God is in heaven. The kingdom is simply the reign of God; it is the exercise of his right to rule. And that is supremely true in heaven.

Unlike Socrates, Christians proclaim that this sovereignty of God has appeared in human history. They got the idea from Jesus. He preached that his power over disease, and demons, and death itself, demonstrated that authority from the Hidden World had appeared on earth. "The kingdom of God," he preached, "has come upon you" (Matt. 12:28). He meant himself. He was more than an envoy of the Almighty; he was the Almighty—in disguise.

He often spoke of his presence as a light in darkness. "I am the light of the world," he said. And he taught his disciples how to share in his mission. "Let your light shine before men,"

183

he told them, "that they may see your good deeds and praise your Father in heaven" (Matt. 5:14–16). They were ordinary men with the common failings of human nature, but under Jesus' influence they became reflectors of his light—envoys of his authority.

That is how the Christian mission began. Today believers look back over two thousand years, but they cannot escape that original mandate: "Let your light shine before men." What did Jesus mean? How are Christians light in the world? How is the kingdom of God infiltrating enemy territory?

The Shape of the World

Christians have not gone into a uniform world. Over the centuries and around the earth today believers have lived and served Christ in a host of circumstances. Their mission is determined in part by the conditions they find in their own world.

Both history and the contemporary scene reveal at least three fundamental conditions into which Christians are sent:

First, in some societies Christians are a small minority and their social influence is minimal. In these countries, as believers are faithful to the gospel their way of life usually provides a sharp contrast with the world around them. They are subject to the same attitudes and reactions of minorities everywhere. But in spite of their limited influence in the political and social arena, their church life is often dynamic and attractive to outsiders. It is often a model of social relationships, reflecting reconciliation and forgiveness under the Lordship of Christ.

In general, this was the condition of the churches in the first three centuries of Christian history. They demonstrated for all subsequent generations of Christians that large numbers and positions of power in society are not essential for influence and impact upon the world.

Second, in other societies churches are a part of a long tradition of Christian influence in public life, in government, politics, and social customs. The acceptance of Christian behavior has become so widespread that a sharp contrast between the lifestyle of Christian churches and surrounding society has almost disappeared. Under these conditions it is not always clear to what degree Christians have "Christianized" society and to what degree society has "paganized" the church. In either case, Christians have access to public office and to other decision-making positions in the society.

These conditions not only prevail in sub-cultures of Christians here and there about the globe today; they were also the social context for the church throughout most of the Middle Ages. The Christian light was so successful in dispelling the darkness of paganism in much of the Roman Empire that men came to talk about Christendom and Christian Empire and Christian nations and Christian culture. This success created Soren Kierkegaard's problem. How do you introduce Christianity to Christendom? Or if we shift the image, how do you let your light shine in twilight?

Third, in still other societies Christians live under the constant opposition of some anti-Christian force. This power is usually some ideology or some religion established by law or tradition. In these circumstances, such as in a communist country or a Muslim state, the Christian mission is often reduced to a struggle for survival and Christians are treated as second class citizens. Persecution, an ever present threat, seriously restricts personal evangelism and public worship.

This third condition is common in the modern period of Christian history when so many political ideologies have arisen to challenge traditionally Christian societies. A sometimes subtle, sometimes blatant barrage of anti-Christian propaganda adds to the church's handicap. This criticism of Christianity is usually based on some real or supposed fault of the church in the past: its imperialism, anti-intellectualism, colonialism, or otherworldliness.

Ideals of the Western World

In many Western countries this anti-Christian attitude comes not in the form of direct attack, but in the quiet displacement of traditional Christian beliefs by secular values drawn from a pragmatic version of humanism. It is not difficult to spot the moral breakdown in the Western world. In the name of personal liberties the public media will often ridicule marriage, while social agencies vainly try to find alternatives to disintegrating families. Most members of society think of life in terms of material wealth and comfort, but find their work almost devoid of meaning.

For millions employment is synonymous with boredom. And leisure hours are seldom filled with healthy recreation; they usually call for some vicious amusement associated with alcohol or drugs—chemical escapes from emptiness and anxiety. The old sense of community has practically disappeared. In most big cities millions live in utter loneliness. And over this whole scene the constant fear of some nuclear nightmare casts a hellish shadow.

What is the answer for this crisis? There is no shortage of proposed remedies. In the so-called "free world" nearly all of them reflect the secular values of the idea of progress: politics, education, and science. Almost everyone assumes that Christianity has nothing to say.

Those who prescribe some political remedy or new legislative diet tend to forget that politics is the art of governing that requires an accurate reading of the people governed. If a political system is unjust, exploitative, and self-serving, it is usually a reflection of the people's own apathy or injustice. Enforcement of laws is limited by public morality. As long as people are greedy, dishonest, selfish, and immoral, no political system can be entirely just. It can only treat the symptoms of social sickness.

To address this weakness in the political system other people look to education to cure society's ills. In any democratic society education has a role to play. Fears feed on ignorance and an informed citizenry is basic to the ballot. But education without faith, informed by a sense of justice, can only develop what is latent. It cannot change human nature. It can make a saint into an intelligent believer, or it can make a thief into a crafty burglar. It can teach the young to read the classics or to pour over pornography.

Practically the same criticism applies to science as a remedy for the moral crisis. Science has provided us with cures and comforts beyond the highest hopes of our ancestors. But as we have discovered, scientists can also refuse to assume responsibility for the results of their research on the grounds that politics and morality do not fall within the realm of science. Science is supposed to be indifferent to moral considerations. It doesn't care whether a laboratory produces penicillin or plutonium, whether a computer stores literature or lies.

The nuclear age has headlined this ecstasy and agony of science and raised a troubling question in the minds of common folk about the control of any science that endangers their lives, be it nuclear fission, genetic engineering, chemical contamination, or any other.

Light in the Darkness

The Christian response to this moral crisis in the Western world is neither a program for a new society nor a withdrawal into an inner world of the spirit. Today as always Christians serve as light in the world. They insist that social problems are often moral problems because human beings are bound by moral laws and societies must respect them.

If a community is to be healthy, it must recognize the sanctity of life, marriage, and property. Leaders must administer justice impartially. People must consider promises binding. The state must be the servant of the people—not their master. It must make virtue easier than vice and punish crimes against its citizens.

This is no exhaustive list. It cannot be because Christianity advocates no specific political program. Political needs vary from age to age; but Christianity is a way of life for all generations. It has grown through a host of political and social conditions. As G. B. Caird once said, as conscientious citizens, Christians are bound to take an interest in politics, but their Christian faith will not automatically tell them how to vote.

On rare occasions, a political issue may be so clear that all

Christians ought to rally to one side of a dispute. But usually all available policies are imperfect by Christian standards, so equally loyal and sincere Christian citizens will arrive at conflicting convictions.

Christians are light in this darkness in two basic ways: First, they influence society at large by the light of the gospel. Second, they build the church, a special community in society.

Christians as light in the world means that they face two basic responsibilities: They must keep the darkness from extinguishing the light and they must extend their light into wider and wider realms of darkness.

The Christian usually lives in a world that repudiates his faith and his behavior. We have come to call this resistance to the light "peer pressure." The pressure appears in small matters. In the neighborhood, on the job, or in public schools the Christian rubs shoulders with people who drink too much, tell sexually suggestive stories, sanction racism, and steal other people's property.

If the Christian refuses to condone immorality or dishonesty, he often finds himself the target of ridicule. Immoral people always resent the example of moral people. A Christian's mere presence is a silent criticism of a questionable lifestyle, and a non-Christian never feels comfortable until the Christian offers some symbol of his approval of the immoral action. As a result, the non-Christian is always pressuring the Christian to accept his sin. Evil is contagious. The Bible puts it bluntly: "Bad company corrupts good character" (1 Cor. 15:33).

Social pressure can make life miserable for adults, but its greatest impact is on children and adolescents, who have less resistance to this kind of coercion. Many a teenager has sacrificed his future and his health to avoid the rejection of peers. Christian parents who try to raise their youngsters by Christian values find that other children are often their most vicious opponents.

Fortunately, social pressure is never irresistible. The apostle Paul encouraged the Corinthian Christians with a reminder that temptation is common and God will not permit a believer to be tempted beyond what he can bear. God himself provides a way to stand up under it (1 Cor. 10:13). All great social advances have come from men and women who were unwilling to follow the herd.[1]

Respect for Life

Resistance of the darkness, however, is the least part of the Christian's life in the world. Christians have proved time and again that darkness can be turned to light. The world can be changed. Two examples from the past will demonstrate how Christian values can shape society.[2]

Take, first, the attitude toward life itself. In 1897 scholars unearthed the rubbish heaps of Oxyrhynchus in Egypt. Among the finds was a letter from an ordinary man of the first century. His name was Hilarion. He wrote to his wife Alis: "If—good luck to you!—you do have a baby, and it is a boy, let it be. If it is a girl, put it out." By "put it out" Hilarion meant to get rid of it. Now this is not a criminal talking. Hilarion seems to be an ordinary decent citizen, even a loving husband. His attitude toward infanticide was common.

The same pagan attitude toward unwanted babies appears in Plato. In the *Republic* he sketches a society, not as it was, but as it ought to be. In this society marriages should be sacred. But what in the name of sanctity does Plato propose for marriage? He recommends that "the offspring of the inferior, or of the better when they chance to be deformed, will be put away in some mysterious unknown place, *as they should be.*"

Contrast Plato's attitude toward infants with Jesus' attitude. Jesus called little children to him, set them in the midst of his disciples, and said, "The kingdom of God belongs to such as these" (Mark 10:14). The disciples did not miss his point.

In an early church manual called the *Didache* we can catch the Christian attitude: "Thou shalt not murder a child by abortion, nor kill one when it is born." Again in an anonymous letter to a man named Diognetus, written in the second century, the author describes the life of Christians: "Christians are not differentiated from other people by country, language or customs. . . . They marry and have children just like everyone else; but they do not kill unwanted babies."

Christians held that taking the life of an infant was sin. They knew that life is from God and eventually the Roman world agreed with them. For the first time, in A.D. 374, it became a crime in the Roman Empire to take the life of a child.

In modern times this ground had to be won anew by Christian missionaries who went to countries where the gospel had not yet penetrated society. Early in the nineteenth century, William Carey, the Baptist minister, campaigned against the sacrifice of infants in the rivers of India. Later in that century, Mary Slessor, the Scots missionary, resisted the ritual murder of twins in Calabar. Examples from other countries abound.

The respect for an infant's life in many cultures today is due at least in part to Christian influence. We have come to take many of these ideals for granted, but a good share of them owe their origin and spread to the Christian faith. The gospel brings a new tenderness to life.

The second example is Christianity's struggle against slavery. Many Americans are familiar with the Christian defense of slavery in the old South. But this conservative reaction to the challenge of abolitionism is only a small episode in the Christian story. It is a reminder that the struggle included, at times, opposition from within the Christian camp. But Christians' reflection of their own cultural setting in no way negates the argument that Christian light can penetrate the world's darkness.

The social system of the Roman Empire at the birth of Christianity depended upon slavery for nearly all of its labor, skilled and unskilled. Edward Gibbon estimated that at the time of Claudius (A.D. 41–54) slaves made up half of the population in the Roman world.

The overthrow of that gigantic evil could not come overnight. Christians, in fact, like those in the old South, were part of the system. Not only did Christians live in a society supported by slaves, but large numbers of them were slaves. Their critics claimed that they preached to the dregs of the population and that slaves were the means of Christianity's spread to other members of a household—carriers, as it were, of the disease.

The way the faith first modified the system is illustrated beautifully by Paul in his letter to a Christian master. He urges Philemon to receive back a runaway slave, now converted, "no longer as a slave, but better than a slave, as a dear brother" (Philem. 1:16).

In a world half slave, half free, no one inside or outside the church thought of the instantaneous overthrow of the system. In the church, however, believers took equality for granted. Inscriptions on early Christian tombs almost never indicate a freeman or a slave. When the great persecution of the church swept across the empire, mistress and maid were confined to the same prisons and died in the same arenas.

The crumbling of the system in society did not begin until Constantine's conversion (A.D. 312) made official enactments against slavery possible. And other factors made them sensible. The first meager legislation against it is striking. It forbids the branding of runaway slaves on the face because "the face is formed in the divine likeness." Other ameliorating acts followed one by one. During these years the churches continued to insist that in Christ "there is neither bond, nor free" (Gal. 3:28, KJV). In one sermon on baptism from the fourth century we can readily capture the attitude.

Gregory, pastor of the church at Nazianzus in Asia Minor (today's Turkey), told his people: "Do not, you rich, disdain to be baptised with the poor, nor you noble with the base, nor you masters with one till now your slave. . . . From the day that you are born anew, all the old marks disappear."

In the church "the old marks" may have vanished in a new birth, but in the Roman world they took a little longer. By the time of Emperor Justinian (A.D. 525)—after two hundred years of the Christian Empire—Christians at last succeeded in convincing Roman society that slavery was contrary to God's creative purposes.

Colonies of Heaven

This light upon the darkness of child abuse and slavery would have been impossible had there been no church to sustain it. The overthrow of evil came because individual Christians reinforced one another in the fellowship of the saints and because the Christian faith, nurtured in the community of believers, made this overthrow possible. The light of God's truth shines brightest in the church.

Jesus did not say to each disciple, "You, my friend, are the light." At times that may be true. The believer may have to stand for the truth alone. But he is always supported by the people of God who share the same unique quality, the power to illuminate darkness, made possible by contact with the Light. Jesus wanted to stress that corporate reality, so he said, "You (a plural pronoun) are the light of the world" (Matt. 5:14).

It is true that churches are often far from models of the kingdom of Light. They are composed of struggling pilgrims on the way to the city. They have not yet arrived, but they have heard the good news of the Kingdom. Jesus Christ is Lord! So the church serves as a colony in which a believer can practice his faith, freed from unnecessary peer pressure and supported by a company committed to the same way of life and the same homeland. This image of kingdom, colonies, and pilgrims was familiar to early Christians. They could hardly escape it.

When Augustus became the first emperor of Rome (27 B.C.), Roman armies had conquered a territory stretching from the North Sea to the Sahara desert, and from the Atlantic Ocean to the river Euphrates. Within these borders peoples of many races and languages lived and worked in various states of culture, from the barbarism of central Europe to the educated elegance of Greece.

Such an empire was won by force, but power alone was unable to unite it. Augustus saw that his only hope of maintaining imperial authority over this vast conglomeration lay in joining its diverse population by bonds of common interest and common loyalty. He had to spread Roman law, Roman culture, Roman ideas, and the Roman way of life throughout the provinces.

In the past, Rome had settled communities of army veterans, called colonies, as garrisons in conquered territory. Augustus extended this practice by giving full Roman citizenship not only to settlements of veterans but to important provincial cities and to men who had distinguished themselves in public service. These provincial communities held equal rights and privileges with the citizens of Rome itself. In return they were expected to represent Rome and all things Roman to their neighbors, so that the Roman way of life might permeate their province. This policy proved extremely successful. In A.D. 212 the Emperor Caracalla was able to issue a decree admitting all his subjects to Roman citizenship.[3]

During New Testament times the city of Philippi, where Paul founded a church on his second missionary journey, was a Roman colony. When Paul later wrote to the church at Philippi and underscored the meaning of church membership, he had at hand an illustration his readers could easily understand. "Our citizenship," he wrote, "is in heaven." James Moffatt translates the statement even more strikingly: "We are a colony of heaven" (Phil. 3:20).

We can easily extend the image: This world is an empire; its capital city is heaven; its emperor is Jesus Christ. But the Lord Jesus Christ has not yet subjected the world to his law, educated it in his ways, or united it in loyalty to himself. To achieve all this he has set throughout his empire colonies with all the rights and privileges of the kingdom of heaven and with his own authority and power at their disposal. Their responsibility is to represent the Lord and the Christian way of life to the world, until the light of the gospel permeates society and all men confess "Jesus is Lord."

19

The Point of Providence

"It is sometimes difficult to resist the conclusion," said Malcolm Muggeridge, the indomitable British journalist, in 1974, "that Western Man has decided to abolish himself, creating his own boredom out of his own affluence, his own vulnerability out of his own strength, his own impotence out of his own erotomania." [1]

Before 4000 participants at the International Congress on World Evangelization in Lausanne, Switzerland, Muggeridge traced his experiences in public life going back a half century to World War I. During these years, he said, he was told the war was to make the world "fit for heroes to live in." God was surely on Britain's side and his spokesman, it turned out, was Woodrow Wilson. So in the columns of the *Manchester Guardian* Muggeridge thundered away about how the League of Nations would insure peace if only everyone would disarm and institute democracy and education for all.

That seemed like the wise course to Muggeridge; he had been brought up to believe that the welfare state in accordance with the policies of Britain's Labor Party would bring Jesus' kingdom to earth. When the Labor Party eventually gained ascendency, to Muggeridge's surprise Jesus' kingdom failed to appear.

Disillusioned, Muggeridge turned his hopes for a better world toward the Soviet Union. "Managing to get myself posted to Moscow as a newspaper correspondent," said Muggeridge, "I soon realized that, far from giving a new vitality to liberty, equality, and fraternity, the Soviet regime was rapidly turning into one of the most absolutist tyrannies of history. Thenceforth I had no expectation whatsoever that man could perfect his own circumstances and shape his own destiny."

Who would think of blaming Muggeridge for his pursuit of history's meaning? Here and there a philosopher tells us that history has no meaning. But most people find that courageous skepticism unbearable. Like Muggeridge, they want to find some purpose in human existence. Where, they ask, is history going?

The Direction of History

Ever since the ancient Hebrew prophets found their people trapped between the threatening empires of Egypt and Assyria, people in what we have come to call Western Civilization have held that life on planet earth does move with some purpose.

This is one of the major distinguishing marks of the Judeo-Christian faiths in the Western world. They believe that ultimate meaning courses through history. Or to make the point in religious terms, God works in and through human affairs to accomplish his own cosmic purpose. The major Eastern religions do not believe that. They teach instead that men and women must escape from history somehow in order to find life in the realm of the gods.

That is why some have called faith in human progress and the Marxist ideology Christian "heresies." Both teach that life's meaning can be found in history, in the global triumph of democratic ideals or in the socialist state that follows the revolutionary overthrow of capitalism.

Winston Churchill, the redoubtable voice for democracy during World War II, once traced the direction of progressive liberalism in the twentieth century. While addressing the Mid-Century Convocation of the Massachusetts Institute of Technology, he said we entered this terrible twentieth century with confidence. "We thought that with improving transportation nations would get to know each other better. We believed that as they got to know

each other better they would like each other more and that national rivalries would fade in a growing international conscious-
ness.

"We took it almost for granted that science would confer con-
tinual boons and blessings upon us. . . . In the name of ordered
but unceasing progress, we saluted the Age of Democracy express-
ing itself ever more widely through parliaments freely and fairly
elected on a broad, or universal franchise. . . . The whole pros-
pect and outlook of mankind grew immeasurably large, and the
multiplication of ideas also proceeded at an incredible rate."

Unfortunately, as Churchill confessed, this vision was not accompanied by any noticeable advance in the stature of man,
"either in his mental faculties, or in his moral character. His
brain got no better, but it buzzed the more." [2]

The whole liberal vision rested upon an optimistic view of
human nature that brought personal freedoms to masses of people
who had never before dreamed of contributing to their own desti-
nies. Something, however, happened to the dream. As Churchill
said, the twentieth century saw man become "the sport and pres-
ently the victim of tides and currents, of whirlpools and tornadoes
amid which he was far more helpless than he had been for a
long time."

Marxism

Among these tornadoes was the lightning-like spread of Marxism. Masses of people came to believe that Marxism's faith was
more realistic than democratic liberalism. It looked not to humane
politics but to economic laws. It believed in sin, in the enslavement
of the dispossessed, in the exploitation of the poor. It traced
the demon to property. The capitalists, owners of the means of
making a living, were driven by greed to the exploitation of wage
earners, the working classes. Conditions went from bad to worse
until the enslaved masses were driven to revolution, the violent
overthrow of capitalism, and the creation of some socialist regime.

Unfortunately, as Muggeridge discovered in the Soviet Union,
in state after state liberators were quickly transformed into op-

pressors. Sin may have corrupted the old regime; but suddenly it appeared in a new one as well.

The history of the last two centuries will show how often Christians joined Muggeridge in singing the praises of Marxism. All men, including Christians, have a tendency to expect too much from earthly regimes.

The Christian faith has since its earliest days insisted, however, that the significance of history comes not from within the ebb and flow of time but from beyond history. God, who reveals himself to man in creation and the cross, holds the secrets to the mysteries of time.

The sovereign Lord of the universe takes a hand in ordinary history in two fundamental ways: he gives providential oversight to human affairs; and by direct intervention he will bring to an end the course of all human history. The first involves the doctrine of providence; the second embraces the doctrine of eschatology.

Divine Providence

As we have seen, the Living God of the Bible is transcendent. He is the Holy One living in unapproachable splendor. However, he does not govern the universe by remote control. He takes a hand in world affairs and knows the passing thoughts of every man, woman, and child.

The Bible teaches that God is involved in creation, not only in the original act of creation, but in the continuing work of creating. The Old Testament says that every movement of the stars, every change of the weather, every phase of the life cycle of the tiniest creature is directed by God, the Creator.

According to Psalm 104:

> the Lord . . .
> makes springs of water pour into the ravines;
>   it flows between the mountains.
> They give water to all the beasts of the field;
>   the wild donkeys quench their thirst.
> The birds of the air nest by the waters;
>   they sing among the branches.

> He waters the mountains from his upper chambers;
>   the earth is satisfied by the fruit of his work.
>   (vv. 10–13)

This same God, who created and sustains all things, also directs
the affairs of individuals and nations. He is more than an idle
spectator of the human drama; he directs rulers and prompts
people. There is, as Cambridge historian Herbert Butterfield once
said, "a kind of history-making that goes on over our heads."
We call this history-making divine providence: God's guidance
of human events according to his purpose and plan.

The most dramatic depiction of this work of the Living God
is in the message of the Hebrew prophets who spoke of the Assyrian and Babylonian crises. As one empire after another sent
its invaders surging across the barren wastes of the Middle East,
these men of God traced the hand of God in the events.

First came Assyria, marching on northern Israel. And how
did the prophet Isaiah interpret the invasion? In his prophecy,
Isaiah voices the wrath of God:

> Woe to the Assyrian, the rod of my anger,
>   in whose hand is the club of my wrath!
> I send him against a godless nation,
>   I dispatch him against a people who anger me,
> to seize loot and snatch plunder,
>   and to trample them down like mud in the streets.
>   (Isa. 10:5–6)

Israel had sinned; judgment must fall.

Assyria's invasion, then, is more than empire-building, more
than one mighty kingdom swallowing up a helpless smaller state.
According to the prophets, this incursion into Israel's borders
is a "club of God's wrath."

Early Christians read these prophecies and made them a part
of their own Bible. From these Hebrew seers they learned to
look at history morally. Like the Jews before them Christians
believe in a moral retribution at work in the very processes of
time—a kind of judgment before the final judgment.

Judgment in History

This divine retribution appears primarily in the flaws concealed in human political and economic systems. Men create their institutions and for a time they serve the purposes of their designers quite well. But something always goes wrong. All systems face time's withering test and eventually judgment falls.

Time knows no favorites. It has tried a host of political structures: city-states, empires, republics, monarchies, parliaments, dictatorships, democracies, oligarchies. It doesn't seem to matter, for what falls under God's judgment in the course of time is not this or that system, but human nature itself. Man seems to be marred by a fundamental flaw. He cannot realize his own ideals. Time brings out the basic human willfulness and the structure crumbles.

The French Revolution affords a vivid example of how quickly a liberal movement can degenerate into a totalitarian autocracy. Within ten short years after the storming of the Bastille, France stumbled through democracy, a republic, a reign of terror, an oligarchy, and a dictatorship.

The Hebrew prophets taught—and Christians believe—that God's judgment in history falls heaviest on those who think of themselves as gods and fly in the face of Providence by demanding that men worship their way of life. That was Assyria's sin. She had no thoughts of serving God's purposes. She had visions of empires in her brain. Her own right arm had gained the victory.

> As one reaches into a nest,
>   so my hand reached for the wealth of the nations;
> as men gather abandoned eggs,
>   so I gathered all the countries;
> not one flapped a wing,
>   or opened its mouth to chirp.
>
> (Isa. 10:14)

Assyrian arrogance was no frustration for God. Isaiah asks, "Does the ax raise itself above him who swings it . . . ?" (10:15).

As soon as the Lord used Assyria to bring Israel to her knees, he dealt with the haughtiness of her invaders.

Later in the prophetic era came Babylonia, sweeping down on Judah. Like Isaiah before him, the prophet Jeremiah calls Nebuchadnezzar, the king of Babylon, God's *servant* (Jer. 25: 8–9). He came to judge God's people, to bring them to their senses.

This is tough faith. It takes a special kind of person to see the hand of God in the suffering of a native land, especially from an empire that is ruthless or cruel. One prophet, Habakkuk, dared to raise that issue. His problem was that God seemed to wink at the wickedness of the invaders:

> Your eyes are too pure to look on evil;
> you cannot tolerate wrong.
> Why then do you tolerate the treacherous?
> Why are you silent while the wicked
> swallow up those more righteous than themselves?
> (Hab. 1:13)

God never gave the prophet a full answer. He told him that the Babylonian's day will come. Wickedness will not go unpunished. But the Lord has a purpose in the apparent tragedies of life. The man of God must rest assured that these sufferings are not the final answer—that will come in the end. Until then, the righteous man will live by faith in God who is sovereign and just (Hab. 2:2–5).

According to Isaiah, Jeremiah, Habakkuk, and their colleagues, human history is a mighty drama which the Lord God is staging upon the earth. The nations are as a drop in a bucket before God. He raises up one ruler and disposes of another. He is the judge of the nations.

Men, however, have trouble reading the signs of the times. God's wrath and mercy are mingled, so evidence of his judgment is always incomplete. He crushes wrong but new wrongs appear. Only the future will reveal the full meaning of human experiences. God's sovereignty will be evident only in final judgment and renewal. History must find its meaning in its end.

History's Last Word

The term for this view of history is eschatology. It comes from the Greek word *eschaton* meaning "last" or "the end." So the eschatological view of history stresses the conviction that God has the last word about history. In terms of the familiar spiritual: "He's got the whole world in his hands."

In the end God will manifest himself to all in a dramatically new way. The Christian holds that the meaning of history—human destiny, if you please—does not arise from within history itself. It must come from God, who participates in history but who stands outside the human story.

Jesus introduced an unusual explanation of this sovereignty of God in his teaching about the kingdom of God. Jewish teaching of his time stressed a two-age view of history. This age is under the authority of evil powers: sin and death and the devil. So men live in frustration and fear. But another age—the age to come—will someday break upon the people of God. The Messiah will appear to free his people from the shackles of fear, oppression, and death. Then they will know the peace and righteousness of God's kingdom.

Jesus apparently accepted this widespread Jewish view (Matt. 13:22) but when he spoke of the kingdom, he gave it a strikingly new twist.

The expressions the "kingdom of heaven" and the "kingdom of the Lord" went back to the days of Israel's most illustrious monarch, King David, whose reign became a token of the Lord's rule. In the Psalms and the words of the prophets, God's covenant and promise to David point to the Lord's own faithful rule and the hope of the coming "advent" (or appearance) of the Lord's anointed servant—the Messiah.

Jesus drew upon this faith—not without some risks of misunderstanding—when he announced "the kingdom of heaven is at hand." He made it clear that the kingdom came to men; they do not create it. Men and women need not ask, "How can we establish the kingdom?" Their first concern should be, "How do I enter the kingdom? Am I ready for the kingdom?"

Jesus answered that question for his disciples by pressing the essential importance of faith in him. That was the surprisingly new note. Jesus indicated that his miracles and message were signs that the age to come had already appeared! Peace and righteousness of the kingdom were already available to anyone who trusted him for liberation from moral failures, and evil powers, and fears of death.

At some future day this kingdom, this sovereignty of God, would be manifest for all to see, but for the moment any genuine believer, any person trusting in him for deliverance, could find a foretaste. So according to Jesus, the kingdom is already present in human history and yet it will come some day in evident glory.

Martin Luther captured the idea for Christians when he paraphrased the Lord's Prayer, "Thy kingdom come, thy will be done" (Matt. 6:10):

"Grant that this Thy kingdom, now begun in us, may increase, and daily grow in power. . . . Help us that we may remain constant, and that Thy future kingdom may finish and complete this Thy kingdom which is here begun." [3]

Christians have not always taken Jesus' message in this eschatological and intensely personal way. Some have tried to turn it into middle class moral counsel, others into a plan for social revolution. But for most, Jesus' teaching, like his death and resurrection, is directed at the struggle of the soul in every age of history.

The most influential interpretation of human destiny in Christian history comes from an age of crumbling empires. At the dawn of the fifth century men expected the Roman Empire to endure forever. They called it "eternal" Rome. Suddenly, however, in the year 410, a barbarian warlord named Alaric besieged the city. All cries for mercy proved futile. Alaric and his Visigoth warriors charged through the gates and plundered the capital, palace by palace.

A short time later, when the hordes withdrew from the city, devastation and ruin were everywhere. Shocked refugees fled in all directions. Some of them arrived in North Africa where they were welcomed by a slim figure with sharp features, Aurelius Augustine, the Bishop of Hippo.

As always in an event of that magnitude people cried out for explanations. "Why? How could this happen? Were the gods angry? Is this a sign of the end of the world? What went wrong?" To answer such questions and give his people a reason to go on, Augustine set about to give an explanation for the rise and fall of empires—and the personal pleasures and tragedies of life. We call his book *The City of God*.

Augustine's interpretation reaches back into the distant past— to creation itself—and forward to the final hour of the human story. In this cosmic context he discovers two realities which unite and divide all history, two historical societies or cities, now mingled by world events but destined one day to be separated. Like Jesus' kingdom, then, Augustine's city is eschatological. History is determined by destiny.

What is the difference between the cities? It is a difference of faith and love. "Two cities," writes Augustine, "have been formed by two loves: the earthly by the love of self, even to the contempt of God; the heavenly by the love of God, even to the contempt of self. The former, in a word, glories in itself, the latter in the Lord. For the one seeks glory from men; but the greatest glory of the other is God, the witness of conscience."[4]

Christians hold that all institutions of history—empires, religions, nations, families, tribes—are subordinated to the central issue of all history: How does a soul appear before God? Is it enslaved to personal passions and pride or does it know the liberty of new loyalty to God? As Augustine, the great North African, put it in one sentence: "In this mortal life a man is trained for eternal life."

Alternative Ways

The Christian view of history which focuses upon the liberation of individual souls and the creation of a destined community rejects two popular alternatives: the belief that the meaning of life comes in some escape from history, and the belief that history provides the whole story of reality. Christians reject all escape routes from history as well as all utopias in history.

The view that men must find reality outside history is very

common. According to Christopher Dawson, the influential Catholic historian, "This denial of the significance of history is the rule rather than the exception among philosophers and religious teachers throughout the ages from India to Greece and from China to Northern Europe."[5]

The escapist view is basic to most forms of Hinduism and Buddhism. If God is the constant Being, as compared to an incessantly shifting realm of human experience, then God, not history, must hold the meaning of existence. So to seek reality, man must carry the soul beyond time into the Great Other World.

The Christian faith shares with this escapist view the conviction that there is more to reality than we see. History itself does not contain all of history's meaning. Meaning, however, will not come from any journey of the soul beyond the particularities of human existence to some realm of universal truth. God's kingdom is not of this world, but it has nevertheless come to time and space. It is, in an important sense, part of our history. Jesus Christ was crucified under Pontius Pilate. The gospel is good news about events in time.

The second alternative to the Christian view, the belief that history holds the answer to life's mystery, is likewise common. It appears most often in some form of imperialism, either religious or political.

The ancient Roman Empire, for example, claimed to embody the meaning of human history. Major literary figures in ancient Rome speak repeatedly of the empire's "eternity" and "finality." Vergil, Polybius, and Livy consider *Roma Aeterna* the culmination of a secular process.

Early Christians, however, were convinced that Rome was not eternal and consistently rejected Rome's pretensions to divinity. They did so because they knew that God alone, the Lord of all history, was worthy of worship.

And that is the same conclusion Malcolm Muggeridge reached. He, like millions of Christians before him, turned from the dreams of democratic societies and the nightmares of communist regimes and found life's meaning in Jesus Christ.

20

The Final Curtain

After World War II Arthur Miller's play *Death of a Salesman* turned the spotlight on the emptiness of American values. Willy Loman, the salesman, was a backslapping, life-of-the-party type. He drifted through life convinced that to know the right people and to be well liked was the formula for success. He lived by this creed; he taught it to his sons. He carried the deception almost to the end. Before he died, however, his business associates, his boys, and even Willy himself, saw through the charade. He died an empty, broken man.

A newspaperman once asked Arthur Miller how he explained the power of the play. He said the story dealt with a problem we all face, "the fear that one has lied to one's self. . . . What the play does is to make the individual ask himself whether his rationalizations about himself are not leading him to an ultimate rendezvous with a dreadful reckoning." [1]

Eschatology

In the Christian vocabulary the word for this rendezvous is eschatology. It is the doctrine that God determines human destiny. Whatever other powers we may meet in this life, God's power is final. He has the last word. Simple reflection will show that men and women encounter "the end" in two ways: in personal death and in history's final curtain. There is a personal end and a cosmic end.

Willy Loman is not alone. In our day men try in countless ways to camouflage death. We try to pretend that it is not a reality. We disguise it with our clever euphemisms. To avoid the term "death" we substitute "passed away" and for the cemetery we speak of "perpetual family plots." When a loved one dies we pay cosmeticians handsomely to make our relatives look "natural" just before we lay them to "rest." All of our games, however, fail to hide the harsh fact of death.

Man is mortal. That is rock-bottom reality. From the moment of birth, he is on his way to death. Perhaps the ancient prophet in Israel put it best: "All flesh is grass" (Isa. 40:6). It springs up, dries in the heat of the sun, and is soon swept away and forgotten. Death is the only prediction we can make about human history with absolute certainty.

Men look at death in several ways. Science tells us that it is a natural thing. All living organisms die. Why should the human species escape organic disintegration? Man simply shares mortality with parakeets, roses, and beagles.

Most of us, however, know instinctively that death is more than a biological fact. It frightens us. The thought of death, our death, brings a sense of dread. We long to cling to life and we consider death an intruder. It seems to rob us of everything worthwhile.

When the Bible calls death an "enemy" we know exactly what it means. It is an enemy, a vicious, dreaded enemy. What power, we ask, has written this irrational end into the human story? If death means that it is all over, why is the longing to go on echoing in my heart? Life on earth cries out for some sequel.

This yearning for life after death is all but universal. Not many people are willing to accept death in a matter-of-fact way. Sigmund Freud called the belief in life after death "the oldest, strongest and most persistent wish of mankind." You can find it in nearly all the world religions, ancient and modern.

In Hinduism men and women look for absorption of the individual soul into the world soul. They think of it as a drop of water falling into the ocean. In most traditional religions of Africa death is an unnatural event. The disembodied soul joins the spirit world, waiting to enter another body. In most religions life after death is shrouded in uncertainty, but it is a reality.

Among the ancient Greeks, life after death was linked to the immortality of the soul. They held—and many moderns share their view—that human beings are made up of two essential parts, a body that will be buried or burned at death, and a soul that will survive the trauma called death. The soul is the indestructible component of human nature. It will live on in some shadowy existence after death.

In spite of what many people think, Christians have never shared this pagan view of immortality. The Christian view of the afterlife is shaped by Jesus Christ's attitude. In the four Gospels Jesus dominates death. He submits to it, but only on his terms. He was sent into the world, he says, to change the face of death.

Upon hearing of the death of one of his closest friends, a man named Lazarus, Jesus told his disciples that Lazarus was "asleep" and that he would go and wake him. When he arrived in Bethany, he told Lazarus's two grieving sisters, "I am the resurrection and the life. He who believes in me will live, even though he dies." Then, as though demonstrating his claim, he raised Lazarus from death (John 11:17–44).

Jesus claimed to control even his own death. He said he had power to lay down his life and power to take it again. He convinced his disciples, and he did just what he said. By rising from the grave he revealed his power over death. That is what sent his disciples out preaching of Christ as the way, the truth, and the life of the Hidden World.

In Christianity, then, man is not by nature "immortal." God alone possesses "immortality." He alone dwells in "unapproachable light" (1 Tim. 6:16). In the Christian faith man's immortality is not innate; it is a gift from God available through Jesus Christ. He brought "life and immortality to light through the Gospel" (2 Tim. 1:10).

The Return of Christ

Nowhere do Christians differ more sharply from their secular neighbors than in their special view of life and death. Apart from the Bible, modern men are inclined to think of man as alive as long as he moves about in some degree of health. When his health begins to fail seriously, people say that a man is dying.

The Christian, however, gives a sharply different meaning to the words "life" and "death." A man may be dead in the midst of life; or he may be alive in the midst of death. That is because death is linked to sin and spiritual life is found in a restored relation to God. Death is existence in evil; life means communion with God.

For the Christian, physical death is a step into life. It is not a terminus, but a transition. It leads to a fuller experience of life with God.

In one of his books, A. M. Hunter, the New Testament scholar, relates the story of a dying man who asked his Christian doctor to tell him something about the place to which he was going. As the doctor fumbled for a reply, he heard a scratching at the door, and he had his answer. "Do you hear that?" he asked his patient. "It's my dog. I left him downstairs, but he has grown impatient, and has come up and hears my voice. He has no notion what is inside this door, but he knows that I am here. Isn't it the same with you? You don't know what lies beyond the Door, but you know that your Master is there." [2]

The approach of death often raises questions in people's minds. Sometimes Christians ask: What about those who die before the return of Christ? Do they go to be with Christ as soon as they die, or do they wait around in some disembodied condition until the resurrection when Jesus returns to earth?

That sort of question assumes that conditions after death are essentially the same as on earth. As far as we are able to determine, however, life beyond death is beyond the earthly measurement of time. So any discussion of how much time elapses between death and resurrection is beside the point. All who die trusting in the Lord Jesus Christ die in his love and will probably be unconscious of any passage of time before Christ's return. The image of sleep that Jesus used of death is helpful here. Most of us are not conscious of the passing of time between our going to sleep and our waking in the morning.

In the one passage in the New Testament which offers an answer to believers troubled about their dead loved ones, Paul writes: "The dead in Christ will rise first. After that, we who are still alive and are left will be caught up with them in the clouds to meet the Lord in the air. And so we will be with the Lord forever" (1 Thess. 4:16–17). What Paul stresses here is not the condition of the soul between death and resurrection but the result of resurrection—believers will be with the Lord forever.

In another letter Paul applies this truth to himself. "I desire," he says, "to depart and be with Christ" (Phil. 1:23). That sounds like Paul expected to be with Christ immediately after death. But later he writes: "We eagerly await a savior from [heaven], the Lord Jesus Christ, who . . . will transform our lowly bodies so that they will be like his glorious body" (Phil. 3:20–21). That suggests that believers will not be raised up for the new life of God's kingdom until Christ returns.

On the surface the two statements appear contradictory, but we must remember that earthly time is irrelevant beyond death. The Christian believer awaits the day when time itself will be taken up into God's eternity, when Christ will come to call to himself all who love him, both the living and the dead. So the timing doesn't matter. What does matter is Christ's triumph over death.

God's Ultimate Triumph

The Christian faith stresses not only man's personal destiny, revealed in his death and his life after death; it also speaks directly to mankind's cosmic destiny.

The question has assumed unusual significance in the late twentieth century. The spread of environmental pollution, the constant threat of nuclear radiation, and the rapid depletion of the earth's resources, all these keep the question of man's ability to survive on planet earth at the center of public attention. Along with its stress on man's stewardship of the earth, Christianity offers a constant reminder that history's finale is in God's hands.

Over the years Christian believers have tried to picture this ultimate disclosure of God's plan for the ages. In recent generations some have tried to draw up a calendar of the end-of-time events, much as one would plot the course of a war after the fact. Most Christians have confessed several major features of the end without attempting to treat biblical prophecy as one would human history.

The Apostles' Creed, confessed by Christians over the centuries and throughout the world, is content to speak of four aspects of the end of the age: (1) Jesus Christ shall come to earth again, (2) he shall judge the living and the dead, (3) men will be raised to life, and (4) Christian believers shall receive "life everlasting."

These four aspects of the end are related to each other because they all relate to Christ and the gospel. Through his death and resurrection Jesus anticipated the final unraveling of history's mystery. But only at his return to earth will his work as the mediator of salvation be complete. It seems best to let these four major convictions guide our thinking along with Christians in other ages.

If we ask where Christians got the notion that Jesus Christ will return to earth some day, the answer can come from only one source. Jesus himself taught his disciples to look for his return. Mark 13 and its parallel passage Matthew 24 are filled with traditional Jewish images and are therefore difficult to interpret in every detail, yet the basic point comes through clearly. Jesus expected to return to earth after his original departure and he taught his disciples to look forward to that event. He linked it with the end of the world as we now know it.

In these passages Jesus underscored two themes: No one knows the exact time of this great event, but the primary responsibility of a disciple is to be ready for it. He must take the promise seriously and live in the light of it.

The New Testament writings themselves reveal how intently

the early disciples looked for the coming of their Lord. They were a generation of believers on tiptoe. Their worship services were celebrations of his presence and promised appearing. Their preaching to the pagan world was fired by the hope of Christ's coming to right all wrongs and to overcome man's last enemy, death.

In the light of Jesus' teaching and the faith of the first disciples, the important question about the end is not "When?" or "How?" but "Who?" Who will be in control of human destiny? Who will be in charge when the secrets of men's hearts shall be revealed? There can be only one answer to that question: Jesus Christ.

When Jesus Christ returns he will complete his work of salvation by triumphing over the last enemy. He will give to all his people transformed bodies. Christian believers will be changed and made ready for the life to come.

Christians have always found a sure promise of this event in Jesus' own resurrection. The apostle Paul wrote that Christ had been raised from the dead as the guarantee that those who sleep in death will also be raised (1 Cor. 15:20).

The apostle explained that the generation of Christians who are alive on the earth when this occurs will not die, but will simultaneously share in the transformation of their bodies. This glorification—as Christians call it—is necessary, because our present corruptible bodies of flesh and blood cannot inherit the incorruptible kingdom of God. So Paul declared: "Listen, I tell you a mystery: We will not all sleep, but we will all be changed—in a flash, in the twinkling of an eye, at the last trumpet. For the trumpet will sound, the dead will be raised imperishable, and we will be changed. For the perishable must clothe itself with the imperishable, and the mortal with immortality" (1 Cor. 15:51–53).

This is the way John Donne pictured the event in his "Holy Sonnet VII":

At the round earth's imagin'd corners, blow
Your trumpets, Angels, and arise, arise

From death, you numberless infinities
Of souls, and to your scatter'd bodies go,
All whom the flood did, and fire shall o'erthrow,
All whom war, death, age, agues, tyrannies,
Despair, law, chance, hath slain, and you whose eyes,
Shall behold God, and never taste death's woe.

Christians hold that the relation of the resurrection body to the earthly body is one of continuity and transformation. In his first letter to the Corinthians the apostle Paul compares the human body to a seed which is transformed into a flower. It is sown in one condition but it blooms forth in another—continuity but wonderful transformation.

The best illustration of the change is the risen Jesus. He was different. The two who walked the Emmaus Road with him did not recognize him. When he took bread to break it, however, he was known to them in the breaking of bread (Luke 24:30–31).

Apparently, life in the world to come demands similar "spiritual bodies," personalities suited to a spiritual environment. Christian believers will not be mere shadows of their former selves, nor physical copies. They will be changed, transformed for life in heaven. As David Winter says in his book *Hereafter,* "Just as the caterpillar has to be changed into the butterfly in order to inherit the air, so we have to be changed in order to inherit heaven."

The Vindication of Justice

Christ's return will bring judgment as well as resurrection. The life to come demands not only transformed bodies; it requires the vindication of justice.

Few would deny that life in this world is unjust. The rich exploit the poor, the ruthless terrorize the humble, and the powerful abuse the weak. Lovable children are denied a stable home and capable couples are unable to have children. Tyrants die peacefully in their beds while saints sometimes pass in agony to the stake. Clearly, man knows no universal justice on this earth. The most massive injustices go unpunished, and the most admirable unselfishness goes unrewarded.

Yet the instinct of justice remains strong in all of us. One of the first things a child learns to say is, "It's not fair." We spend our years appealing to some abstract principle of justice that we feel in our bones and assume that everyone else feels too. Nationality, politics, and culture make no difference. Communists, atheists, humanists, and Christians make the same appeal: "It's not fair." And yet we all recognize that, in the final analysis, this life is not fair. Even with the best intentions in the world, human justice is fallible.

How can a God who is almighty and good possibly allow this pervasive injustice to continue? If he does nothing, either now or after this life, to correct this gross unfairness and dethrone the reign of evil, he is either not all-powerful (and so cannot do it) or he is not good (and so does not care). But if he is all-powerful and good—which is what the word *God* means to most of us—then it seems he must act to put things right. Justice on a cosmic scale must prevail and must be seen to prevail, or God is not God.[3]

Obviously, God has not yet established justice on earth. So the strong presumption is that he will establish it after this life is over. That is what the Bible teaches. Paul wrote to the Thessalonians: "God is just: He will pay back trouble to those who trouble you and give relief to you who are troubled. . . . This will happen when the Lord Jesus is revealed from heaven in blazing fire with his powerful angels" (2 Thess. 1:6–7).

The theme of the final judgment of God, in which the mighty are dethroned, the proud are scattered in the imagination of their hearts, the rich sent empty away, and the good who are hungry and poor are exalted, runs strongly through the teaching of Jesus and the apostles (Luke 1:51–53). We might think that God is blind to human injustice, but one day mankind will see that he cares intensely about it, and the inequalities and evils of life on earth will be put right.

Henry Wadsworth Longfellow affirmed the triumph of divine justice in these familiar lines about the meaning of Christmas:

> I heard the bells on Christmas day
> Their old familiar carols play,

And wild and sweet the words repeat
of peace on earth, good will to men.

And in despair I bowed my head:
"There is no peace on earth," I said.
"For hate is strong, and mocks the song
Of peace on earth, good will to men."

Then pealed the bells more loud and deep:
"God is not dead, nor doth He sleep;
The wrong shall fail, the right prevail,
With peace on earth, good will to men."
—*I Heard the Bells on Christmas Day*

Jesus described the final judgment in terms of a shepherd separating the sheep from the goats (Matt. 25:32). However much it may offend liberal sentiment, the Bible indicates Jesus believed and taught that people could be excluded from the future life with God.

That negative note, however, is not the dominant theme of the New Testament or of the Christian faith. The resounding melody of the New Testament is not death and despair, but life and hope. Christ has come and will come again. And that truth, Christians have always confessed, gives us reason to sing.

21

New Day Dawning

Above the altar, at the far end of the Sistine Chapel in the Vatican stands Michelangelo's massive painting of *The Last Judgment.* High in the center of the scene sits Jesus Christ, his right arm raised in vigorous, decisive judgment of the earth's peoples. Below him heavy figures of the condemned tumble uncontrollably downward toward the darkness of perdition, while the figures of the blessed sweep upward to join the angels in the realms of Light.

The Christian vision of the world to come is so grand, so all-encompassing, so awe-inspiring that only a Michelangelo or a Dante or a Bunyan dare trace its boundaries for the human imagination. Human words simply fail and even artistic genius falters when men contemplate the Christian vision of the life to come.

So when we ask what Christians believe about the life to come we recognize the limitations of all human descriptions. Christians only dare to speak because God has revealed the reality. The Bible, they contend, teaches that the "life everlasting" is the fulfillment of God's work in time; it is the consummation of his purposes in creation.

Christians are not alone in their hope for a life to come. To the great masses of men, the finite world which impinges upon our senses draws its existence from a realm of reality beyond itself. That is why peoples throughout history, and in non-Western cultures in our own time, look at death with a strange blend of hope and dread.

Archaeologists, digging around in the graves of people who lived ten thousand years ago, have found time and again some object that points to a crude conception of the afterlife: sometimes weapons for the happy hunting ground; sometimes a canoe for crossing to the isle of the blest. But whatever the image, the afterlife is a central part of the religious faith. This life is but a prelude to the next.

Man's Ultimate Choice

The life to come is also central in Christianity. Early Christians stated it simply: "I believe in the life everlasting." But what do Christians expect to find in the life to come?

Unlike the other world religions, Christianity speaks of life after death with a note of certainty. We can trace this certainty, like so many others, to Jesus Christ. He taught his followers about the Hidden World because he said he came from there. And when his enemies hounded him to his death, he arose from the realms of the dead and demonstrated to his disciples his right to speak of the invisible world and of the conditions that they could expect to find there.

As a consequence, Christians have always taught that men have only two fundamental alternatives before them. They either have God—and in him everything eternal—or they have nothing but themselves. One is called heaven and the other hell. Man's choices—arising from the Supreme Choice in this life—determine which it will be for eternity.

Jesus Christ indicated that every day in a host of minute and major decisions people choose death instead of life. They live in the Kingdom of Death instead of the Kingdom of God. Jesus' passion to deliver men from this darkness explains his single-minded purpose. He knew that if sinners did not repent and look to God for his forgiveness, they were already prisoners of hell.

Today it is no longer fashionable to speak of hell. Modern

men have become so sensible, so wise in their own eyes, that any idea of judgment or hell is treated as nothing more than a stage for jokes.

Most Europeans and Americans have been told so often that everyone has a spark of good in him that they have come to believe God will eventually be able in some way to welcome almost everyone to a blissful eternity. And even where people do not share this optimistic assessment of human nature, the thoughts of hell are so widely ridiculed they leave men with the impression that they can take their chances on life after death. "Live for the moment and don't worry about tomorrow."

It should be clear that more than outdated images of hell have been discarded in this secular faith. By rejecting the old images of eternity as grotesque and immoral, people have made the mistake of rejecting the truth. The Christian insight into the eternal significance of the decisions of life has gone as well. Many no longer think of their daily decisions—is it right or wrong?—as anything other than daily decisions. Life is simply lived; it is no longer chosen. As a result, millions endure a meaningless, day-to-day existence.

It is almost impossible to tell whether most people are rejecting some degraded presentation of the Christian faith or the faith itself. But so many ridicule the traditional images that they compel thoughtful Christians to explain their language.

What can we say, then, about the crowns, the harps, the golden streets, and the pearly gates in traditional descriptions of heaven? They are the biblical writer's way of suggesting to the imagination what cannot be put in prosaic terms. They are attempts to express the inexpressible. White robes are symbols of spotless purity, crowns point to moral victories, harps represent abounding happiness, and gold the timelessness of heaven. All these things—purity, moral victory, abounding happiness, permanence—are realities most people crave but cannot find on this earth.

Similar figurative language appears in the Bible when an author speaks of hell. Fire suggests suffering; darkness indicates isolation; a bottomless pit points to abject fear and insecurity. These, too, are experiences in this life, especially when people are enslaved to pleasure and pride and have no room for love in their lives. The language of hell, then, points not only to conditions beyond this life, but also to conditions people can experience on this earth.

Consider the dilemma of the biblical authors. They tried to describe conditions of existence that no man has fully fathomed. And yet they had to draw upon experiences of people in this life to make the other world imaginable.

The Great Divorce

Relying on an assortment of images, Christianity has always taught the reality of hell as well as the exultation of heaven. The term *hell* is the translation of a Greek word in the New Testament, *gehenna,* meaning "valley of Hinnom." Since the second century B.C. the Jews believed that this valley south of Jerusalem—where child sacrifice had once taken place—would one day be the scene of judgment. Open flames would devour the godless. Christians adopted this Jewish word to indicate the destiny of unrepentant spiritual rebels.

Gehenna, however, is not the only term the New Testament uses to designate the fate of the condemned. The idea also appears as everlasting fire, eternal wrath, outer darkness, and "weeping and gnashing of teeth." This suggests that the New Testament is not so much interested in determining the *place* of hell as in indicating the *conditions* under which the condemned are destined to live.

This condemnation should strike no one as a sudden surprise. It is merely the fruit borne of a life cultivated in evil. In his book *The Great Divorce,* C. S. Lewis says the condemned are those to whom God finally says, "Your will be done."

Non-Christians often ask the Christian, "But how can the God of love allow any of his creatures to suffer unending misery?" The question is, how can he not?

The fact that God is love makes hell necessary. "Hell," as E. L. Mascall once said, "is not compatible with God's love; it is a direct consequence of it." That was his way of stressing the fact that the very God who loves us is the one who respects our decisions. He loves us, but he does not force his love on us. To force love is to commit assault. He allows us to decide. He loves us, he encourages our response, he woos us, he pursues us, he urges us, but he does not force us, because he respects us.

God leaves the choice to us. We can either throw ourselves in gratitude into the arms of self-existent Love, or we can repel it in a brutish attempt to affirm our own self-sufficiency. After all, what place could there be in a community throbbing with love for people concerned only to assert themselves?

In Jean-Paul Sartre's play *No Exit,* three characters—Inez, Estelle, and Garcin—find themselves together after death. All of them have died under circumstances that are clearly disgraceful.

In the room where all three are confined, it soon becomes obvious that each of them is interested in the others only as an audience for his or her own attempts at self-justification and displays of self-pity. None of them cares for the others for any other reason. None shows any sign of gratitude or penitence; all are resentful and bitter.

As the play proceeds, it becomes plain that these three persons are doomed to remain alone together throughout eternity. The unheeded arguments repeat themselves in endless circles and the emotional tension becomes unbearable. No sympathy. No love. No community. As the curtain descends on the scene of never-ending and ever-mounting frustration, the inmates sum up the significance of the drama in two desperate exclamations: "We shall be together forever! Hell is other people!"

Significantly, on other lips these sentiments might be descriptions of the joys of heaven. "We shall be together forever"—the communion of saints in the life everlasting.

The Grand Alternative

In describing heaven the Bible sometimes tells us how it is unlike our present life, and sometimes it tells us how it is so much more than this life.

For example, in John's vision of heaven, found in the Book

of Revelation, he hears a loud voice from the throne. It says, "God . . . will wipe every tear from their eyes. There will be no more death or mourning or crying or pain, for the old order of things has passed away" (Rev. 21:4). Heaven is apparently sharply different than the sorrow-filled existence man finds on earth. And that is part of its wonder.

The ancient book of Job says, "Man born of woman is of few days and full of trouble" (14:1). A Negro spiritual echoes this theme but adds the note of release:

> Soon we will be done wit' de troubles of de world,
> > troubles of de world
> > troubles of de world
> Soon we will be done wit' de troubles of de world.
> Goin' home to live with God.

Heaven is unlike earth. That is the point. In speaking of the presence of God, John apparently intended for us to turn sorrow and death and pain upside-down. Heaven, he suggests, will be filled with joy and life and pleasure.

John's vision of heaven, in fact, paints a whole series of contrasts with earth. In contrast to the darkness of most ancient cities, John says heaven is always lighted. In contrast to rampant disease in the ancient world, he says heaven has trees whose leaves heal all sorts of sicknesses. In contrast to the parched deserts of the Near East, he pictures heaven with an endless river of crystal-clear water. In contrast to the meager existence in an arid climate, John says heaven's trees have twelve kinds of fruit growing on them. In a word, heaven is a wonderful destiny free of the shortages and discomforts of this life.

But can we be more specific? How is heaven like life here and now?

The Vision of God

We find a clue in Jesus' beatitude: "Blessed are the pure in heart, for they will see God" (Matt. 5:8). To see God is to live. But what can it mean to see God? A moment's reflection will reveal that it is possible to "see" in several senses. A tourist might drive through the observation point of the Grand Canyon in a half hour. Has he seen the Grand Canyon? A traveler might fly in and out of the airport at Paris. Has he seen Paris? This is not what the Bible means when it promises that the pure in heart will see God.

There is, however, another type of sight. Have you ever noticed two lovers at a sidewalk cafe? They sit for hours, sipping a drink and staring into each other's eyes. They are lost in the wonder of each other. Their highest pleasure is to be with their lover. Surely this is closer to the meaning of "seeing" God. It is the contemplation, the magnetic beauty, the inner delight of basking in the presence of Someone you love.

The Bible makes clear, however, that human sight cannot bear the vision of God. When Moses, the leader with whom God spoke face to face, begged that God would show him his glory, God responded, "You cannot see my face, for no one may see me and live." So God told Moses: "There is a place near me where you may stand on a rock. When my glory passes by, I will put you in a cleft in the rock and cover you with my hand until I have passed by. Then I will remove my hand and you will see my back; but my face must not be seen" (Exod. 33:18–23).

It is true that on occasion, in the Old Testament, God appears to men. But when he does the note of terror always sounds. When Isaiah, for example, saw the Lord high and lifted up in the Temple, he cried out: "Woe is me! I am ruined! . . . my eyes have seen the King, the Lord Almighty" (6:5).

In a similar way, when God appeared to Ezekiel by the banks of the Chebar River, his glory was veiled. What Ezekiel saw was "the likeness as the appearance of a man" (1:26, KJV). Even then, however, the prophet fell on his face in awe at the sight. The message seems clear: to see God is to die.

Something obviously had to be done. That is what the Christian gospel proclaims: God has done something. He has made possible man's vision of God. "No one has ever seen God, but God the only Son, who is at the Father's side, has made him known" (John 1:18). When Philip came to Jesus with the request, "Lord, show us the Father," he received Jesus' reply, "Philip, anyone who has seen me has seen the Father" (John 14:8–9). Men see God, then, in Jesus Christ. That vision is possible now by faith. Heaven is a promise that some day it will be "face to face."

To "see" God in that sense means to love him, to praise him, to enjoy him. It is the end of our selfish search for happiness. It is the homecoming of the prodigal. It is the satisfaction of the thirst that we could not quench. It is the reason for our existence. It is the end of our creation. It is peace, and home, and rest. It is heaven.

Sometimes people ask, "Will you go to heaven when you die?" But a more important question is: "Are you the sort of person to whom heaven would seem desirable?" The choices we make in life are built up into our characters as bricks are built up into a house. They make us the kind of people we are.

G. B. Caird once said, "The man who habitually puts his trust in God and tries to follow in the steps of Jesus Christ will become the sort of person who would be at home in the presence of God. The man who laughs at the gospel, breaks all the rules, and throws away his life in unrepentant waste, will become the sort of person who would be more seriously out of place in heaven than a tone-deaf man in a roomful of musicians." [1] The presence of God would be to him a worse torture than all the horrors of hell.

That is why the Christian doctrines of heaven and hell are so much more than mere doctrines. They are reminders that every day in a host of ways we are all making choices—casting ballots, if you please—for the eternity that awaits us.

> Finish then thy new creation,
> Pure and spotless let us be;
> Let us see thy great salvation
> Perfectly restored in thee!
> Changed from glory into glory,
> Till in heav'n we take our place,
> Till we cast our crowns before thee,
> Lost in wonder, love, and praise!
> —Charles Wesley
> *Love Divine, All Love Excelling*

Notes

Chapter 1

1. Quoted in Louis Cassels's *The Reality of God* (Scottsdale, Pa.: Herald Press, 1972), 13.
2. I am grateful to Harry Blamires for this point about twentieth-century novelists. See *The Christian Mind* (Ann Arbor, Mich.: Servant Books, 1963), chapter 1.
3. G. K. Chesterton, *Orthodoxy* (Glasgow: Collins, 1908), 53.
4. G. B. Caird, *The Truth of the Gospel* (London: Oxford, 1950), 110.
5. Clyde S. Kilby, ed., *An Anthology of C. S. Lewis* (New York: Harcourt, Brace & World, Inc., 1969), 22, 24.
6. J. B. Phillips, *The Newborn Christian* (New York: Macmillan, 1978), 140.

Chapter 2

1. Bertrand Russell in "A Free Man's Worship."
2. Martin Luther, *Epistle to Galatians.*
3. Quoted in Kilby, *Anthology,* 23
4. C. S. Lewis, *Reflections on the Psalms* (New York: Harcourt, Brace & World, Inc., 1958), 116–17.

Chapter 3

1. The story of Bishop Felix is from Herbert Workman's *Persecution in the Early Church* (London: Epworth, 1923), 275.

Chapter 4

1. Langdon Gilkey tells of his experience in his book *Shantung Compound* (New York: Harper & Row, 1966).
2. Aleksandr I. Solzhenitsyn, *The Gulag Archipelago* (New York: Harper & Row, 1973), 168.

Chapter 5

1. I have taken the Stevenson story from Cornelius Plantinga Jr., *A Place to Stand* (Grand Rapids: Bible Way, 1981), 44.

2. Chesterton, *Orthodoxy,* 31.

3. C. S. Lewis, *Mere Christianity* (London: Collins, 1952), book 3, chapter 11.

Chapter 6

1. J. S. Whale, *Christian Doctrine* (London: Collins, 1963), 55.

2. Quoted in Cassels, *Reality,* 42.

Chapter 7

1. The opening story of the battlefield is from Roger L. Shinn's *Life, Death, and Destiny* (Philadelphia: Westminster Press, 1957), 9.

2. Blaise Pascal, *Pensees,* 555.

3. C. S. Lewis, *Letters to Malcolm* (New York: Harcourt Brace Jovanovich, 1964), 75.

4. Thomas S. Kepler, ed., *Anthology of Devotional Literature* (Grand Rapids: Baker, 1947), 377.

5. Normal Snaith, *The Distinctive Ideas of the Old Testament* (London: Epworth, 1944), 102.

Chapter 8

1. The quotations from Charles Templeton are in a news story by George W. Cornell, *The Denver Post,* 19 May 1978.

2. Peter Berger's observation is quoted in Cassels, *Reality,* 14.

3. C. S. Lewis, *Mere Christianity,* book 2, chapter 1.

4. I first saw the argument about the "scale of evil" in E. L. Mascall, *The Christian Universe* (New York: Morehouse-Barlow, 1966), 151.

Chapter 9

1. C. S. Lewis, *Mere Christianity,* book 2, chapter 3. Used by permission of the original publisher, William Collins Sons & Co. Ltd., London.

2. Dorothy L. Sayers, *Creed or Chaos?* (New York: Harcourt, Brace and Co., 1949), 24.

3. Michael Green, ed., *The Truth of God Incarnate* (Grand Rapids: Eerdmans, 1977), 26.

Chapter 10

1. C. S. Lewis, *The Lion, the Witch and the Wardrobe* (Middlesex: Puffin Books, 1950), 148.

2. Harry Blamires, *On Christian Truth* (Ann Arbor: Servant Books, 1983), 52.

3. I have drawn the argument about psychic phenomena from Michael Green, *The Truth of God,* 54–55.

4. The argument about the resurrection as a "hoax" is from Caird, *The Truth of the Gospel,* 86.

5. James D. Smart, *The ABC's of the Christian Faith* (Philadelphia: Westminster, 1968), 46.

Chapter 12
1. J. A. Findlay, *A Portrait of Paul* (London: Epworth, 1936), 102.

Chapter 13
1. Dorothy Sayers uses this analogy of creativity in one of the more insightful discussions of the doctrine of the Trinity. See her book *The Mind of the Maker* (New York: Harper & Row, 1941).

Chapter 14
1. Mike Yaconelli, *Tough Faith* (Elgin, Il.: David C. Cook, 1976), 31.
2. The position we take in this chapter, stressing the church as a community of faith, is akin to the evangelical tradition rooted in the Protestant Reformation of the sixteenth century. Many other Christians hold the "catholic" position which stresses the essential role of a divinely appointed priesthood in defining the church.

Chapter 15
1. The reader must note the way I have raised the question. The Bible, the message preached, and the sacraments are ways the Word—the revelation of God—comes to us. Obviously, there are distinctions between the "forms" of the Word. First, God revealed himself in special actions and words in history. Then, under the Spirit's guidance, prophets and apostles wrote it down. Finally, the church listens to the Word and teaches it today. The priority here is important. See Shirley C. Guthrie, Jr., *Christian Doctrine* (Richmond, Va.: Covenant Life, 1968), 80–82.
2. Elton Trueblood's comparison of fire and evangelism is in his book *The Incendiary Fellowship* (New York: Harper & Row, 1967).

Chapter 16
1. Used by permission.
2. C. S. Lewis's quotation about decent eggs is from his *Mere Christianity,* book 4, chapter 8.
3. The Paton incident is found in A. Bernard Webber, *More Illustrations and Quotable Poems* (Grand Rapids: Zondervan, 1945), 47.

Chapter 17
1. The Jonathan Edwards's quotation can be found in *Conversions,* edited by Hugh T. Kerr and John M. Mulder (Grand Rapids: Eerdmans, 1983), 69.

2. Adolf Deissmann discusses this concept in his book *Saint Paul: A Study in Social and Religious History* (London: Hodder and Stoughton, 1926), 140–57.
3. I found these lines in A. M. Hunter's *Taking the Christian View* (Atlanta: John Knox Press, 1974), 83.

Chapter 18
1. Many of the ideas in the sections *Ideals of the Western World* and *Light in the Darkness* came originally from Caird, *The Truth of the Gospel,* 150–62.
2. I have drawn the argument about care of children and slaves from John Foster's fine article "Achievements of Christ in Twenty Centuries" in *The Coming-of-age of Christianity,* edited by Sir James Marchant, (Westport, Conn.: Greenwood, 1971), 1 ff.
3. I am also indebted to G. B. Caird for the analogy of Roman colonies and the church in society. It is found in *The Truth of the Gospel,* 159–62.

Chapter 19
1. The address by Malcolm Muggeridge is found in *Let the Earth Hear His Voice* (Minneapolis: World Wide, 1975), 449–56.
2. Quoted in Roger L. Shinn, *Christianity and the Problem of History* (New York: Scribner's, 1953), 4.
3. Quoted in Shinn, *Problem of History,* 77.
4. Augustine, *The City of God,* I, 29.
5. Christopher Dawson, *The Kingdom of God and History* (New York: Willett, Clark & Co., 1938), 198.

Chapter 20
1. Shinn, *Life, Death, and Destiny,* 84–85.
2. Hunter, *Taking the Christian View,* 58.
3. This argument is drawn from David Winter, *Hereafter* (Wheaton, Illinois: Harold Shaw, 1972), 82–85.

Chapter 21
1. Caird, *The Truth of the Gospel,* 126.

Index